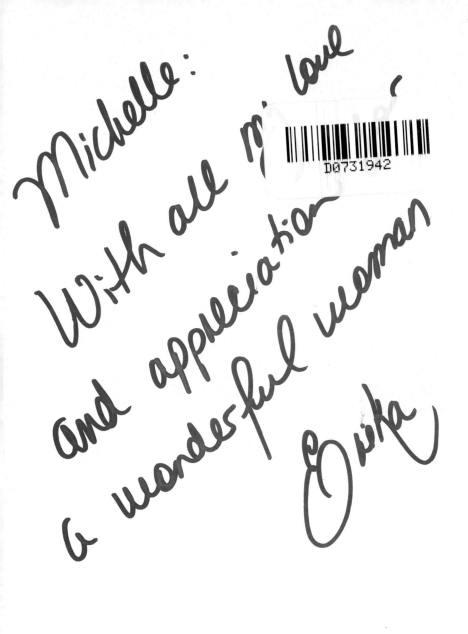

Michelle:

With all my love
and appreciation
a wonderful woman

Erika

D0731942

Beyond

THE LIES

Beyond

THE LIES

THE WAY WOMEN SACRIFICE
FREEDOM BY RELYING ON OTHERS

ERIKA FERENCZI

Beyond The Lies ~ The Way Women Sacrifice Freedom
By Relying On Others

ISBN number: 978-0-9977132-0-6

Printed in the United States of America.

DEDICATION

I want to dedicate this book to the most important people in my life.

To my husband Oscar and my children Elizabeth and Alexander, for being the reason behind everything I do every single day. I am grateful for their comforting presence in my life - for being with me when I am lighthearted and playful, at my best, as well as when I am stressed out and not very fun to be around. I thank our Creator every day for having all of you in my life. Your smiling faces make all the sacrifices worthwhile.

To Andrew and Claudia, my other two children. You will never know how much we love you and the big emptiness we feel each time you leave home. Wish we could have you with us on a constant basis.

To my mother, Rachide: Mom, you have shown me how to be strong, to persevere, and to stand up for myself. You have also shown me that there is nothing more important than our children, but that they should never come before us. You have always been there for me one way or another. I even remember you saying once, "I will always be here for you. I will help you stand up and overcome whatever challenges you encounter. I may get mad and point out your mistakes later, but not before I help you out of your mess. You can always trust in me." I want to thank you, Mom, for always keeping your word and being there for me no matter what. That has been the best gift you have ever given me.

To my father, Juan Jose: Thank you, Dad, for showing me your immense capacity for loving another human being. You have revealed to me just how beautiful life can be, and you taught me that happiness lives within ourselves, no matter what is happening around us. Thank you also for your patience, your life lessons, and of course for always being there for me and believing in me... even when I may not have believed in myself. I hold your teachings close to my heart and always will. I wish I could have spent more time with you, especially when I was little. But life is what it is, and I know now that you did the best you could. I love you, Dad.

To my grandmother, Wahibe who passed away a few years ago. "Taita," as I called her, was the foundation that kept me strong, the inexhaustible source of love, patience and care. This amazing woman showed me love and forgiveness, and I am who I am today in great part because of her. Thank you, Taita - we will be together again some day. But until then, you will always live in my heart.

CONTENTS

Beyond the Lies.

ACKNOWLEDGEMENTS

The list of people to thank is very long, and I hope I don't forget anyone. There are many people who have touched my life in many special ways, and I want to thank all of you.

I want to especially thank people who have played a very significant part in my life and without whom I am not sure I would be here today or what turns my life would have taken.

David Neagle: David, thank you for being yourself with me and for motivating and inspiring me to be the individual I so wanted to be. No other person has had the impact you have had on my life. You showed me how believe again when I had almost given up. Thank you for your belief in me, for your wisdom, and for your willingness to challenge me beyond what, at times, felt humanly impossible to achieve. Thank you for helping me turn my life around. I am living my best life in great part because of you and your work.

Suzanne Evans, Larry Winget, Paige Stapleton, Bryan Stark and the whole SEC Team. Thank you for showing me the way, for walking the path with me, and showing me how to walk it myself. Thank you for your willingness and commitment to excellence, no matter what. You supported me when times were tough and celebrated with me when times were great. Thank you for the guidance, the motivation, and the teachings on how to make what was once a far-off dream a spectacular reality.

Maria Cecilia Orozco: Thank you for opening the doors to your office and to your heart. Thank you for helping me move through one of the toughest moments of my life. Without knowing it, you saved my life in more ways than one.

Kristen Perdue: You have been a steady and strong mentor. I appreciate your wisdom, your infinite knowledge and all the love, support and guidance you have continued to offer over the past ten years. Thank you for your infinite willingness to help me become the best I can be at any given moment. Thank you for being my rock, my guide and my friend.

Jennifer Barley: Jenn, you motivated me in more ways than you can imagine. Thank you for your support and the willingness to stand up for me and my dreams when I did not know how to do it on my own. Thank you for being my friend and for being part of my "anabolic team."

A special thanks to Caroline Allen and Patricia

Beyond the Lies.

Melnyk for helping me make this book a reality. Both of you have played an instrumental part in my journey.

Thank you to all who constantly motivated me and helped me be a better business owner, woman, mother, leader and human being. I could not have done it without you.

THE LIES

THE WAY WOMEN SACRIFICE THEIR FREEDOM BY RELYING ON OTHERS

PREFACE

This is not a book about investing or saving a buck. This is not about making men the enemy, or blaming men for what's going on in the world. This is not a book about investing strategies or the financial system.

This is a book about women's strength and women's inner power.

This book is about much more than money. It is about the sense of security, self-esteem, self-worth, and character that is created when a woman is in charge of every aspect of her life, including her financial situation. It is about giving women back the right to be independent, free, and strong human beings.

This book is about helping women take a stand in their lives, make powerful decisions, and stop apologizing for who they are, what they think, or what they want. This book is about helping women stop trying to fit in and conform to the norms in exchange for love and financial security.

This book is about helping women become unapologetic for who they are, what they want, and helping them live their lives under their own terms.

This book is for the woman who is tired of her circumstances and is determined to change them. This is for the woman who is tired of having someone else tell her what she can and cannot do.

- She is a stay-at-home mom who wants to take charge of her money but does not want to abandon her children.

- She is a woman who wants to start a business because of the flexibility, but she is afraid to take the first step or does not know where to start.

- She is a woman who is searching for a way to be financially independent and still be there for her family, especially her children.

- She is a woman who understands the power and importance of raising strong, empowered, independent, heart-centered, compassionate human beings of the future. She knows that for that to happen, her constant presence and love is indispensable, but at the same time, she is not willing to sacrifice her life in the process.

- She is a woman who has some sort of financial security. Maybe she has started a business but still has not found the way to fully monetize her expertise.

For centuries, women have bought into the fairytale that putting someone else in charge of their financial destiny is safe and okay. I am here to tell you it is not, and that nonsense has to stop!

Fifty percent of first-time marriages end in divorce. That statistic increases to 67 percent for the second marriage and 73 percent for the third, so the odds are not better the second or third time around.

Even if they do stay married, women generally out-live their husbands by six to seven years. And three out of five women over 65 cannot afford to pay for their basic needs and end up becoming a burden to their children.

The statistics:

- **60%** of all young women have experienced physical abuse
- **90%** of women have experienced either physical or emotional abuse
- **82%** of families led by a single woman have no financial stability
- **85%** of the victims of domestic violence are women

If that was not strong enough:

- **50%** of men who abuse their wives also abuse their children
- **69%** of sexual assault victims are under the age of 6!
- And **73%** are under the age of **12**
- **60%** of abused women say they don't leave the relationship for lack of financial means
- **3 out of 5 women** over 65 cannot pay for their basic needs

Clearly there is something wrong with this picture. When did we embrace the belief that letting someone else be in control of our finances or our life is okay, or safe? The facts are telling us it is not.

Most women have been taught by society, by social norms, by their peers and by other women, that they should be looking for someone to "protect them", a strong, wealthy or successful man (or all of the above) as a solution to all of their problems.

They fail to tell you the statistics mentioned above. **They fail to tell you the reality which lies beyond the dream and the happily ever after.**

Women have to embrace, once and for all, that the

moment they give the keys to their life to someone else, then they are giving up their power to choose. They are giving up their freedom, and they are giving up their self-esteem.

Searching for a man who can take care of your needs and believing that will be the solution to your problems is wrong. Most likely marrying such a man is the beginning of even bigger problems.

You may wake up one day to a relationship that's on the rocks, without money, and with little to no self-esteem. Angry. Depressed. Lonely and broke, wondering what went wrong? How is it possible you ended up here?

The truth is that whether you realize it or not, the decisions you made along the way have defined you. Those decisions were made day in and day out and became second nature to you, so much so that they happened without you noticing them. Those decisions have brought you to where you are today.

When someone or something else is in control of your money, they take charge of your sense of security and self-esteem, and if you are a mother, they are in control of your children's security and sense of self-esteem, too.

Your insatiable need to find somebody else to take care of your financial needs is leaving you heart broken, lonely, angry and broke. This book attempts to wake you up and help you avoid becoming another statistic.

This book is a wake-up call to the women of the world. Do not wait until it is too late - until a tragedy happens, or you get sick end up alone – too late to understand that you should have been in charge of every aspect of your life. The truth, my dear, is that until you do, you are not free.

I am writing this book in the hope that it helps you become the strong, confident, unapologetic, heart-centered, empowered and free woman you need to be to help this become a better world.

I am writing this book in the hope that you become **a woman who can be in charge of every aspect of her life and truly become the master of her destiny and the director of her life.**

Welcome to my world!
Erika Ferenczi

INTRODUCTION

There is a moment in every person's life in which the reality they are living is dramatically different from the reality they were expecting to live - dramatically different from the expectations they had for themselves. It has happened to you, to me, and to every single human being on this planet.

At that moment, the way in which you try to understand your situation, the decisions you make, and the actions you take will determine both the quality and the form of your destiny.

Initially, we often believe we are powerless to change our circumstances. Nevertheless, we try to find a solution and continue seeking until we seem to run out of solutions. The endeavor feels so overwhelming that we eventually start to lose hope.

Erika Ferenczi is here to tell you that until you reach the moment in which you say "Enough is enough" - that is, you become dissatisfied enough with your circumstances that you make an unequivocal decision to change - nothing will change in your life.

In *Beyond the Lies ~ The Ways In Which Women Sacrifice Their Freedom By Relying On Others*, Erika explains that no matter how sad or discouraged you are or how many people you blame or complain to, nothing will change unless you change yourself.

The good news is that making a change is not rocket science, and in fact, it is absolutely possible. This is because you *do* have the ability to achieve the financial and emotional freedom you desire, or anything else for that matter, if you make the decision to act and are willing to do whatever it takes to succeed. The bad news is that no one will do it for you. It is you who must make it work. Remember that the only one responsible for your results is you.

Nothing will happen until you take full responsibility for everything you have, feel, think, say and do. No one knows this better than Erika Ferenczi, who went from being a depressed, unhappy, overweight and short-tempered individual to a successful entrepreneur running her own thriving business, living a fulfilling life, and becoming financially independent ... all while empowering the women she works with to do exactly the same.

Beyond the Lies.

Erika Ferenczi takes a

Direct, Blunt and Honest

approach to solving your issues, building a business, and changing your life.

If what you are looking for is someone to complain to and commiserate with, you won't find it in *Beyond The Lies*. What you will find, however, are concrete steps, hands-on strategies, and proven recommendations that you can use to build a successful business and live your best life by changing who you are from the core of your being.

Erika includes very specific exercises and activities at the end of each chapter because there is nothing she wants more than to help you get ahead in the game of life and success. And if you are serious about changing your circumstances, if you are willing to do the work, and if you are willing to start paying attention to the lessons in each chapter, then you are guaranteed to make extraordinary changes.

To experience extraordinary results, you need to **become extraordinary** yourself.

CHAPTER ONE

ENOUGH IS ENOUGH

"There is a difference between giving up
and knowing when you've had enough.
The first one turns you into a loser,
the latter one turns you into a champion."
- Erika Ferenczi

We all get to a point in our lives where we don't like our situation. Maybe we don't like our financial situation, the quality of our health, the nature of our relationship, or the work we're doing.

First, we start complaining then blaming, being dissatisfied, and telling the whole world how miserable we are. Unfortunately, while we're complaining and blaming, we're failing to take action to change the situation.

I have lived in seven different countries, relocated more than ten times, lived among the wealthiest people in each one of those countries, and related to the people with less means, as well. The tendency is always the same. Whether we want to acknowledge it or not, no matter what financial bracket you are in, if you are financially dependent on someone else, the consequences to your self-value, self-worth, freedom and self-esteem are steep.

Unfortunately, instead of taking measures to change their circumstances, women have the tendency to mull over what they do not like for months, sometimes even years. Within this inability to make a change, there are deep-seated feelings of hopelessness and a loss of confidence. Can they make their life work without someone else telling them what they need to do?

The sad reality is that being a victim is far easier than taking charge and changing those circumstances. So most women opt for what they think is easy… sacrificing their own lives.

The first tendency is to find people to "relate to" in our dissatisfaction, people you can complain to and with, most of the times other women, who unfortunately cannot be of much help since they are in the same situation. You may get together for coffee, for supper, for drinks; and the conversation is always the same. It always goes in circles and never ends in a clear solution as to how to get out of the dilemma.

Women can stay in this cycle for years, until the tiredness, the hopelessness, the apparent lack of solutions takes them to a place where they are very close to just giving up.

Beyond the Lies.

They ask themselves:

- How much more will I take on?
- How much more will I accept?'
- How much longer can I take this?

They rationalize:

- It is not that bad.
- Maybe this situation will change.
- I am doing it for the kids.
- I will hang in here just a bit longer.

There is dissatisfaction. There is desire to change. There is this "thinking about it." But still the fear of change is greater than the perceived consequences of what they are living. The problem is they are just looking at the tip of the iceberg without realizing the consequences reach much deeper and farther than what they can see with their eyes, or perceive with their intellects.

This continues for years unless they come to this place in which they truly realize ENOUGH is ENOUGH - until they reach that threshold in which the pain and consequences of what they are living surpass the pain and effort it will take to make a change.

One day the glass overflows. One day, one single thing happens that in the scheme of things may not be so big to the naked eye, but it is the last straw that overflows the glass of water.

When you get to that place, you are at the end of your rope. You feel this imaginary line has been crossed, and you say, "This can't happen anymore. I'm not going to live like this. I have to make a change."

All those years or months of frustration, dissatisfaction, sadness and hopelessness instantly get transformed into anger, conviction, and strength. You feel a commitment towards doing something different and living a different life. Committing, maybe for the first time, to yourself first, instead of towards other's needs and requests.

My Enough-is-Enough Moment

One Sunday morning in the fall of 2005, I was then 31 years old. It was a beautiful morning, sunny, happy, and warm. I was living in Brazil, in a beautiful home I had personally chosen, with tons of windows and light. My bedroom overlooked the pool, and I could see my children playing in the garden from almost anywhere in the house. It was a dream come true. I was married to a very successful man, a great man. I had two beautiful, healthy children - a boy and a girl. I had a stable and abundant financial position. We'd been traveling for six or seven years at that point, living all over the world, experiencing quite a bit of change, relocations, different houses, different cultures.

To everybody, I had the perfect life. Everything looked perfect on the outside. But, the inside was a completely

Beyond the Lies.

different story.

My inner world was completely empty. I was emotionally lonely. I was sad. I was alone. I was very close to giving up. Nothing was working. My marriage wasn't working. We had constant arguments. On good days, we had a cordial relationship at best But most of the time, we had a passive aggressive relationship, and sometimes it was plain unbearable.

Even though I loved my children, I was not being the best mom I could be. In fact, sometimes I was being an awful mom - short tempered, exasperated, at the end of my rope.

All this was normal. It took me a while to understand that it was normal under the circumstances in which I was living. I was frustrated, sad, and lonely. I was having issues in my marriage and constantly wondering when did we make a bad turn? How and when did it get so bad?

When we were traveling, everything was relatively okay. But the truth is that you don't travel all the time. You have to come back home and deal with everyday life. That's when things got really bad.

But I kept telling myself that it was okay, that it wasn't so bad, that I could take it, that I could live like this. I kept telling myself I was doing all this for the kids. I'd ask myself, "How could I be so ungrateful? How could I have everything everybody desired and still be so miserable?"

I put up with the situation for a long time because I didn't want my children to grow up without a family - without their parents or with a divorce – because that's the way I grew up. I didn't want them to experience the same pain and loneliness I experienced as a kid. So I kept telling myself that I was doing the best thing.

Then the Enough-is-Enough moment happened on a regular Sunday afternoon. We were all in the car, the whole family. We had just gotten back home from having lunch. We had gone to this wonderful outdoor restaurant which served delicious food in a wonderful part of town. This particular restaurant was very well known because there is an enormous fig tree in the middle of it. It was a great setting to experience a most fantastic time.

Back at home, while my husband was parking and we were about to exit the car, he and I started to have an argument. The argument may have seemed like any other argument, but this time it took place in front of the children and the nanny who helped us take care of the house. He called me names.

He called me names! I knew that probably in the heat of the moment this was not a big deal because he was used to speaking like that, but for me, it was a big deal.

In that moment, I said to myself, "No more. Enough is

enough. I'm not going to live like this. I'm not going to allow anyone to talk to me like that. I am not going to allow him to treat me like that in front of my children. Or in front of anyone else."

It is important to mention that whenever someone reaches the enough-is-enough moment, what most likely happens is that the person will have no idea about how to get out of the situation in which they find themselves.

In that moment you become crystal clear about what you do not want and very clear that there is something you have to do to change it. But you have absolutely no clue as to where to start.

At this point, it is very easy to get caught up in the fear since we are unable to see "the whole plan" lined up in front of us. Most people stay stuck for many years because they are unsure of how their future will look. In other words, they would like to see the whole solution before they can decide to make a change.

So there I was, clear as day that I could not take the situation anymore. Clear as day that something needed to change, yet afraid and puzzled about what to do next.

I did the only thing I knew to do. I looked at him without saying a word, opened the door, took my children out and thought, "I need to find a solution, and that solution needs to include my two children staying with me. I need to become, once again, the woman who can take care of herself, and now I also have to be able to take care of my two children."

I went into the house, and I did not speak to him for a couple of days until eventually the peace returned. But although there was a temporary peace between us, a line had been crossed. An abyss had opened that would never be closed again.

Today, almost 10 years later I ask you this: What are you waiting for? There is no time to waste. If you are in that situation where you have reached that "Enough-is-Enough" moment, it is time to make a change. No one is comig to save you. The situation won't change by itself. The situation won't change if YOU do not make a change.

If you do not like how you are living, change it.
If you do not like what you are experiencing, change it.
If you do not like how you are feeling, change it.

You are holding the key! The key is in your hands, whether you realize it or not. I know at this moment it may seem like you are not holding the key, but, believe me, you are.

Maybe you are not sure what the future will look like. Guess what. No one is certain until they take the first step. The first step may be simply for you to make the decision and say, "I will not live like this."

Beyond the Lies.

The first step may be to go and buy a book on how to overcome the situation. The first step may be to reach out for help. The first step may be to hire someone who can help you. But what is clear is that you have to take the first step.

Whatever that first step is, make sure you take that step because not making a decision is making a decision in itself. Not making a decision, not taking action, is the same as making the decision to stay exactly where you are.

Many times the best way to define what you want is to be very clear about what you do not want and what you will not tolerate.

When you say "I don't know what the future will look, but what I do know is that I'm not going to live like this." This is your Enough-Is-Enough moment.

I knew for me that time had come. **IT WAS ENOUGH.**

Let's recap:

We all get to a point in our lives, sooner or later, where we don't like our situation. Maybe we don't like our financial situation, the quality of our health, the nature of our relationship, or the work we're doing.

You need to get to the place of saying "ENOUGH IS ENOUGH." You need to get to that place in which making a change is much more important than staying comfortable in the same situation.

There is no time to waste. If you are in that situation where you have reached that "enough-is-enough" moment, it is time to make a change. No one is coming to save you. The situation won't change by itself. The situation won't change if YOU do not make a change.

The only thing that will change your circumstances are the actions YOU take. No one will take them for you. It is not their responsibility. It is yours.

Ask yourself:

→ Am I really at the point where I have had enough, or am I willing to continue to live like this?

→ If the answer is "I am willing to live like this" I would like to ask you: "For how long? How much longer are you going to put your life on hold and let your circumstances deteriorate further?"

→ If you decide "Enough is enough," what is the action you will take today to start making a change?

_____

_____

_____

(Take this space, write it down, and make a commitment to make that change. Not a commitment to me but a commitment to YOU, to your life, to your values, and to what you are worth.)

Do not choose 25 things to do. Choose one or two, and do not stop until you have completed those steps. After that I assure you, the next steps and decisions will be clear to you. But you must take the first step.

CHAPTER TWO
IT IS TIME TO WAKE UP

"The hardest part about letting go is finally realizing there wasn't much left to hold on to in the first place."
-Unknown

Even though I said, "Enough is enough," I truly did not know what to do. I had been in counseling for several years in the different countries in which I had lived.This probably helped me get to this point of change, but I still had no idea what the next steps were. I knew I needed to do something different, but the only solution seemed to be to break up once and for all, without having a plan. I knew I did not want to do that. I had to be smart about it. I had to have a plan.

One afternoon, a friend called me out of the blue, and asked, "When are you finally going to come to one of our meetings?" A group of ladies hosted a meeting every month to create a spirit of support and community. The group would gather at someone's house to drink coffee and eat cake. I usually didn't go because they involved everyone complaining about their situations. I didn't want to be a part of that energy.

This one was going to be different my friend told me. "Someone is going to give a presentation of the book "Women Who Love Too Much." A light bulb went off in my head. I had seen the book before. My mother had been reading it at some point. I felt this meeting was more than about coffee and cakes so I said that I would come.

As I wrote down the time I asked her to sign me up. I felt hope for the first time in a long time. I just knew it was going to be good. Maybe I would meet someone new, maybe a new friend. I knew for sure I would learn something.

As soon as I hung up, I realized I had committed to a meeting at my son's school. And besides I had no way to get there. Brazil was dangerous, and I was not allowed to drive on my own. We had a driver who helped us navigate this complicated city. The problem was that I knew he would be busy that morning driving my husband to a meeting. I was about to cancel when I got this feeling. A guiding voice said, "You have to make this work. You have to make this happen."

That night, I told my husband that I needed to go to the meeting, and I needed to go in a cab. He said absolutely not, that it was impossible, that it was outside of security protocol. I told him I was not sure what the protocol was, but I needed to be there. And I was going to go. I called a friend and asked her if she could pick me up and bring me home. She said yes. I was going to that gathering, and nothing would stop me.

Beyond the Lies.

As it often happens, I learned very quickly - although at the moment I was not conscious of it - that when an opportunity arises, an obstacle will also appear almost immediately after the opportunity. It's as if the universe is testing your commitment and your desire to move forward.

Opportunity is rarely (I would like to say never, but let me be conservative here and say "rarely") convenient. Still, when you know that you need to do something, even if you are not entirely sure why, you should do it. It is better to move forward, no matter what!

On the day of the meeting, I entered the room afraid. I did not know the women. I did not know the presenter. I did not know what I was doing there. I went in, got a coffee so my hands would not be empty, and sat down at the very back of the room, alone. I had women around me, but I was too afraid to speak to them.

Less than five minutes into the presentation my wheels were already spinning! It made so much sense!! The message was about how women "lose" themselves when they compromise, and compromise, and keep compromising in favor of everyone else. It deeply resonated with me.

I was the woman who had left her job, her home, her country, her financial stability, her friends, and her life to follow the man she loved around the world, follow him with the promise that everything would be ok. He would be there all the time, and our love was so strong that it would stand the test of time and any other adversity. After all, he was "the one," wasn't he?

Well, guess what. The dream did not come true. And now, for the first time, I was beginning to understand why. I had compromised. I had compromised once, and twice, and a million times since the moment I decided I wanted to make our relationship work. And I lost "me" in the process. No wonder I was feeling frustrated.

In that moment I understood that the problem was me. Not that my husband didn't have a problem, but I had allowed this to happen. My decisions had gotten me to where I was. No one forced me. No one put a gun to my head. I made the decision!! And now it was time to take responsibility.

I realized not only had I made the decisions but my life was not getting any better. In fact, it was not going to get better unless I did something and did it fast. If anything, the situation was going to get worse. That day really was my wake-up call.

Beyond the Lies.

I asked myself:

- What am I doing?
- What is truly happening here?
- What are the consequences all this is having on my children, my family, and in my life as a whole?
- Where do I want to be 5 years from now?

I knew that I did not want to be this person any more. I needed to change, and I needed help. I could not do it alone but had no idea of where to start either. I just knew there was a problem. I needed to find someone who could give me a guiding light. And in that moment, I realized that I had been guided to come to this meeting. The person in front of me must be able to help me. She delivered the message. She must have the solution, too.

So I approached her at the end of the seminar and introduced myself. I asked her if I could have her contact information and if she was taking any clients. She graciously gave me her contact details, but said she was not taking on anyone new. I thanked her.

I left the meeting, knowing I had to do something. A couple of days later, after thinking about it some more, I called her, talked to her, and again asked her to please see me. If she could not help me it was ok, but maybe she knew someone who could.

I spent more than two hours with her. I don't think I

stopped crying from the time she opened the door to the moment I left. It took me the entire session to explain what was happening. As I told her the story, I discovered new feelings, situations and thoughts I did not even know I had.

I'd fought so hard to keep them down, to keep them quiet. Now they were out, and God, it felt so good. It was such a relief to acknowledge what was truly happening to me. When we finished, I am not sure what situation she saw me in, but it must have been pretty bad because she accepted me as a new client.

I am not sharing her name with you for confidentiality reasons. But she is reading this book, and she knows exactly who she is. I have to tell you she saved my life; she was an angel sent from the sky to shine a light onto my dark path. I am not sure where I would be without her, and I will be eternally grateful to her for opening the doors to her life, to her heart, and to her brilliance.

I believe every single one of my mentors, my teachers, the people I have learned from in my journey to freedom, has been an angel. They were sent to me at the perfect moment and for the perfect reason.

So many times I see people complaining. "This person did not help me." "That other person did not help me either." I have not found one single interaction with a mentor or teacher that hasn't helped me.

Beyond the Lies.

If you are one of those people who perceive it is a waste of time investing in help, the problem may very well be your approach, not necessarily the mentors themselves.

I am sorry to tell you this, but it is the truth. I believe we can not move forward if we lie to ourselves.

Once I heard one of my mentors tell a person the following:

She was complaining about a person not being able to help her, and the another person not being able to help her either, and another person the same. We were in a conference room with around 250 people, and this particular woman was at the microphone asking for help. My mentor paused and said, "I do not believe I can help you either."

Oh my god, I thought. "What has he just said? Why did he say that?" Later I understood. He was saying exactly what I am saying to you today. If you believe no one can help you, very likely no one can, and no one will, because the problem is the way you are thinking not the help those people can provide or not.

Okay. Enough rambling. Back to our story.

Nothing can be changed without awareness. Nothing can be changed without knowing what is happening. We all need to reach the point where we see our reality for what it is. We all need to reach that moment of truth where we finally realize what is happening. And, we all need help. We need a guiding light, an objective point of view that helps us move through difficulties.

If you had the solution, you would have already resolved the problem, or you wouldn't even have had the problem in the first place.

So you either spend the next year, or five years, in the same dysfunction that will get progressively worse, or you can get out of your own way and seek help.

Seeking help is of utmost importance. Stop rationalizing. Stop pretending things are good. Pretending only makes things worse. Be willing to pay the price both emotionally and financially that needs to be paid in order to get the help you need.

Many times paying for that help may seem steep. You are not seeing how much steeper it will be if you go on in life without making the changes you need to make.

You will experience all the consequences, all the pain, all the time wasted in the process of trying to find out the solution by yourself. I can assure you these will be far steeper than whatever it may cost you to move forward.

Not only that, but unfortunately, when you are in a hot

mess, you are in the problem itself, and the way to solve that problem is not necessarily within your realm of consciousness. If it was, you would have solved the problem a long time ago.

I hope you get the strength to recognize that you need help and the courage to seek that help. There is nothing as valuable as that.

Stop lying to yourself. I know you are not doing it on purpose. Very few people do. Usually it is an incapacity to see things as they truly are. Obviously the situation in your head has a beginning, middle, and an end, and in order to make sense of it all, you rationalize. The problem is that you are shortsighted in your own diagnosis of the situation mostly because you are in the situation.

The truth is that the amount of forward movement you can make will always be directly related to the amount of truth you can accept about yourself and your situation without shielding yourself behind a lie.

It is impossible to change a situation if you are not crystal clear on where you are and what is actually happening. As long as you keep pretending everything is fine, as long as you keep lying to yourself, nothing will change. The sad truth is that when you lie to yourself, you allow others to do the same.

It is TIME TO WAKE UP.

LET'S RECAP:

When an opportunity arises, an obstacle will also appear almost instantaneously. It is as if the universe was testing you your commitment and desire to move forward.

Opportunity is rarely convenient. Still, when you know you need to do something, even if you are not entirely sure why, you should do it. It is better to move forward, no matter what!

You are where you are in your life because of the decisions you have made. You made those decisions. You were part of the equation, and until you take full responsibility, you are not equipped to change your circumstances. So let's do it today. Take responsibility.

We all need to reach the point where we see our reality for what it is. We all need to reach that moment of truth where we finally realize what is happening. And, we all need is help.

Stop rationalizing. Stop pretending things are good. Pretending only makes things worse. Be willing to pay the price that needs to be paid in order to get that help.

The amount of forward movement you can make will always be directly related to the amount of truth you can accept about yourself and your situation without shielding yourself behind a lie.

It is time to wake up.

Ask yourself:

→ If you are fully responsible for your situation, what decision do you need to make today to start changing your circumstances?

→ What are you doing with your life?

→ Where do you want to be 5 years from now?

→ What actions do you need to take today to get yourself there?

CHAPTER THREE
STOP BLAMING

"In a state of blame you will never change your life whether you blame something external, or even yourself. In a state of blame you will never change anything."
- Anthony Robbins

Stop blaming others…that is the key to your success. It is as simple as that, and as complicated as that. It's simple to say, but difficult to achieve without daily introspection, awareness, intention, and action.

I know that for the longest time I was blaming everything and everyone around me.

When things don't go our way or when we are dissatisfied or unhappy, we immediately try to look for an explanation. Our minds try to make sense of what is going on around us, so we can "understand" it and make decisions on how to change.

Unfortunately in that quest for truth, we focus where we should not - outside of ourselves. As human beings, we have a default tendency to look to the outside. We haven't been taught to look inside first.

For the longest time, I was blaming everything. I guess I was actually trying to make sense of my circumstances, trying to find out what went wrong. What did I not do? What did I do wrong? I was seeking a solution. Pretty normal behavior. The problem was that I was looking outside of myself -- what my husband did not do, what my parents did not do, what the economy was or wasn't doing, what the government was or wasn't doing.

I blamed the fact that I left my country. I blamed the fact that I wasn't working. I blamed my husband because he had caused all the relocations. I blamed him for not giving me more attention, for not giving me the love I needed, for not being the man I wanted, as if it was his obligation to be the man I wanted. Back then I was dissatisfied, I was angry. I was hurt. I was sad.

I blamed my mother for raising me the way she did. I blamed her for not being there for me as a child. I blamed the situation because I did not have her close by as an adult.

Beyond the Lies.

I blamed my father because when I was a child he left, and then he had another family. I felt he had not been very present in my life.

I blamed everything and everyone. I tried to make all of them change, all of them understand what they had done wrong, and change who they were. I guess I just wanted to be heard, to be understood, and to be loved. I guess I just wasn't feeling loved. It took me a long time to understand that love is not something you can get from the outside. Yes, people can love you and demonstrate their love and appreciation for you, but when your inside is empty, when you on your own have not been able to "fill your own bucket of love," if you will, no matter how much love, time, appreciation and dedication the people around you demonstrate, it is impossible for you to feel "satisfied."

There is always this constant sense of "I do not have enough; I'm not being loved enough, not being appreciated enough, not being heard enough, not been cherished enough. This comes from a deep internal emptiness, an emptiness that cannot be satisfied by another human being.

Feeling a sense of contentment, satisfaction, and internal peace can only come from the ways in which you learn to meet your own needs, to be there for yourself, present in your situation, in your emotions, in your circumstances, without the need to flee, without the need to cover your feelings up or bottle them down… I knew I had a long journey ahead of me….

I arrived at my therapist's office on a wonderful summer day, a Tuesday. The sun was shining; it was warm, but not too hot. There was a certain sense of peacefulness in the air around me.

I remember getting to the building and the garage door being opened. It felt as if I was entering the aisle of hope, the aisle of possibility. I went in, parked the car and slowly climbed out. I looked around me and became present in the moment as to what was actually happening around me.I was feeling hopeful for the first time in a very long time, determined to continue the journey although I was not sure where it would take me. I jumped into the elevator and pressed the button for the 11th floor.

She opened the door as she always did, with a smile on her face, a big beam of bright light coming from the windows behind her. The place was always quiet. There was a sense of peace, security and happiness surrounding her. It took me a while to understand how important those feelings were.

I knew the moment the door closed, I would be heard. I was going to be understood, and I was going to be gently guided through the next step. What that was, I had no idea, but I had to trust. And I did.

Beyond the Lies.

She sat in front of me on an ivory sofa. Her office WAS very different from a normal therapist's office. It was light, very clear, very inviting. I loved coming to her place. She had a beautiful terrace. Sunshine and bird song came in from the terrace.

I was telling her all the things that were going wrong in my life. Complaining, complaining and complaining ... about my mother, about my father, about my husband, even about my children. Of course, in my mind I wasn't complaining. I was just sharing my very clear and vivid reality. I was not aware that what I was actually doing was complaining and giving my power away. But as I was speaking to her, I started actually listening to myself, and how, from my point of view, everyone else was wrong.

Then she told me, in a very loving way: "I hear everything you're saying, and I am truly sorry that you're experiencing this degree of pain, Erika. Rest assured we will find a solution. But Erika, the solution does not lie in the outside or through trying to make others change. Will you trust me enough to look inside at what is actually happening with you?"

She paused, and I nodded trying to comprehend the depth of what she was sharing. She continued, "If so, I promise you we will get to the point of healing and overcoming all these circumstances that are causing you so much pain.

Because the truth is that you're doing the best you can. But for now, please trust me and be willing to walk this path with me. I will guide you, but we have to start with you. Will you trust me? Are you willing to do the work?"

"Absolutely!" I responded. I was committed to doing the work, although at the moment I had no idea what "doing the work meant." What I knew, without a shred of a doubt, was that I was willing to do whatever it took to change the situation. .

"The truth is," she said, "the people you're complaining about, they are living exactly the kind of lives they want to live; they aren't complaining. It is you who is not satisfied with the situation, not them. They are not feeling a strong desire or an incentive to change, and until they do, they will very likely not change. The only one here who is dissatisfied is you. They are okay, in a funny kind of way."

The realization hit me like a bucket of cold water. They were happy. The only one that was suffering was me. So clearly there was something wrong here.

It became pretty apparent to me, just by the remark she had made that "If you want to change your situation, the one who has to change is you." I understood that was the only thing I could focus on: what I was feeling, what I wanted to change, and what I wanted to experience. For that I needed to put all my energy into changing my situation, not theirs. She continued to say, "We have to give you the tools to be happy, whether or not anyone around you changes or not. Are you ready?"

Are you kidding me? Of course I was ready; I was not only ready, I was eager! I did not know exactly what that meant, but it felt like a very good idea to me. It felt like I could finally do something about how I was living. That was the first time I had heard someone say "Forget about all the other people, and let's focus on what you want." Hallelujah!

"Yes, I am ready," I responded, "When are we starting?"

"Right now."

I felt true hope for the first time in a long time. I was ecstatic.

Through the work I did with her and the work I have been doing for around twelve years now, I have learned that the journey is about me, not about anyone else.

Nothing is ever about anything but you - what you need, what you want, what you desire, the way you want to live, the life you want to design. I will talk more about this in chapter # 7 where we will discuss the feeling of selfishness that comes up every time we contemplate focusing solely on ourselves. For now let it be enough to know that your life is yours, and thus it is always about you.

Probably by now you are thinking: "What is she saying? That is so selfish."

I know. I have seen this countless times with the women I work with. Feeling selfish is the first thing that comes to mind when someone is saying "Forget about everything else, and just focus on you." I will ask you exactly the same thing she asked me: Are you willing to trust me? Are you ready for the journey of a lifetime? If the answer is yes... let's get this ball rolling!

Making peace with who the people around you are, and coming to a very clear realization of whether you want to continue to live in your current situation or live a different reality is key.

If you come to realize you would rather be living a different reality than the one you are currently experiencing, before changing anything else, I recommend you focus on changing yourself.

Focus on getting yourself to a place of strength - physical, emotional and financial - before you move any of the other pieces on the chessboard.

You need to learn to be strategic in your moves. The specific moves you make when you are thinking about

Beyond the Lies.

drastically changing the way your life looks need to be well thought out and as strategic as possible.

If those changes have to do with relationships, work, or health, you have to be strategic, otherwise life can play a check-mate on you faster than you think possible.

My father once taught me something that may have very well saved my life more than once. As with any piece of advice that really makes a difference, the principle is really simple, and in that simplicity the magic lies.

My father taught me that life is like a tricycle. He equated the three wheels to your family, your health, and your financial stability. When one of them is shaky, the tricycle will have a hard time moving forward, but somehow it can be ridden until you fully inflate that deflated wheel again because the other two axles are maintaining the stability. But when two of those wheels are defective, everything comes to a stall, and it is much more difficult to move forward. It feels nearly impossible.

This concept has carried me through the years and has helped me understand I have to be strategic about the moves I make in my life. I hope it helps you, too. If you want to change your life, be strategic, and make one strategic move at a time.

If any of those three aspects of your life is shaky, focus on getting those strong and stable before you consider changing anything else. It may take time, but not nearly as much as the time, frustration and heartache that it will take you to bounce back if two or more of those wheels become compromised.

Be strategic in your moves.

When I see life I see a chessboard, and I think about the importance of being strategic regarding my moves. When I think of my life I also remember another of the fundamental principles by which I live my life: "Life is game." Whether you realize it or not, life is a game, the most important game you will ever play, but a game nonetheless.

The faster you realize this is true, the better equipped you will be to play to win. Because the truth is that life is a game that cannot be lost, unless you give up, because once you give up the game is over. And that is a whole different story.

So as long as you are alive, the game is still on. The faster you embrace the fact that life is a game, the better quality your life will have and the more focused you will become. You will be able to play to the best of your ability.

Playing your every move to the best of your ability is really all that is asked of you. If you do, you will see tremendous changes in your circumstances.

Beyond the Lies.

In life, there is nothing that is expected from you but to play your every move to the best of your ability, with awareness, with desire to grow, with desire to be more, to have more, and experience more. That is the basic premise of being alive - the desire and commitment to continue growing every single day, playing and enjoying this beautiful game called life.

When you do that and you open yourself to trust, the next step in your journey becomes really apparent in an effortless way.

After that session with my therapist, I began to wake up, but it still took me quite some time to fully understand how all the blaming was not going to get me anywhere. It took me some weeks to understand it intellectually and has taken me many years to understand and live by the principle that I cannot and should not try to change anyone else.

The desire to change the outside world keeps coming up once in a while, but now it is easier for me to snap out of that idea faster than ever before.

Society, the media, and even Disney World keep telling us that if we can do this thing or if we do that other thing, that person we so much care about might change. In other words, they are like that because you are not doing something. That is the main reason why so many women end up believing they are not enough.

For example the woman who is betrayed by her husband. She ends up believing that if she was enough, he would have never cheated. Or the woman who thinks that if she could only be "funnier" someone else would like her better,etc. You can certainly relate to this, or maybe you have seen a woman, a girl, a teenager going through this vicious cycle.

Well, I am here to tell you that this notion is absolutely false.

You may learn to manipulate people to do what you want once in a while, but as a result of that, the other person will learn to manipulate you to act the way they need you to act so they can feel comfortable.

At the end of the day, you will both lose. Realizing your relationship has turned into a game of manipulation is never fun, even when it was unintentional.

Please do not go that route. A life of manipulation is a life of bondage, intrigue, lies, and loneliness. Please do not play that game. At the end the only one who loses is you.

The only possibility you have of someone else changing is by <u>changing the way you relate to them</u>.

When you change the way you're showing up in your

relationships, when you change the energy you are putting into your interactions, when you change the words that are coming out of your mouth and the intention behind them, when you change your expectations about what needs to happen externally for you to be happy, and when you focus instead on what you need internally, only then will you see change.

It is difficult to make a profound, dramatic and lasting change in yourself when you're dedicated, committed, convinced, and invested in making that change. It is even more difficult to get somebody else to change if he or she does not want to change.

That is why getting someone else to make a profound change is simply impossible. With enough force, manipulation, complaining, and bitching, you may get them to experience a temporary modification in the way they act and react, but I can assure you, if you do not change, they will just go back to the previous way of being. That is where they feel comfortable, that is what they know and do effortlessly. So they will eventually slip back, and there is not a thing you can do about it but bitch and moan some more, which will only make YOU unhappy.

It doesn't matter if you're blaming a person, a thing, or an external situation. I don't care what that external thing is.

Remember: "In a state of blame you will never change your life." Anthony Robbins

As long as you are blaming somebody else, that other entity, individual or situation has power over you.

And what is worse, the moment you need someone to do something so you can have an experience, so you can feel something, so you can be happy or content or satisfied, in that same moment, all the power of your feelings, your success, and what you want is being put in the hands of someone else. Unfortunately this is the fastest way to become completely disempowered over your ability to direct your life.

When you feel there is something external that needs to change, that needs to be modified, that needs to be fixed so you can live life the way you want to, most likely you'll be waiting for things to change, waiting to see if the change will actually take place, and requesting, blaming, and demanding that that change take place.

The fundamental problem is when you demand people to comply with your wishes, they will sometimes comply temporarily, but the truth is that you will never know if they comply out of necessity, because that's truly what they wanted to do. Whatever change is achieved will not be a lasting change. Most likely the person will revert to the original behavior, leaving you even more frustrated, more hopeless, and in the same or worse place than you were to begin with.

Beyond the Lies.

When I finally said "enough is enough," and I started to see the consequences that my actions and my decisions were creating, I began to ask myself the following questions:

- If nothing else changes, if I assume no one around me will change, what do I need to do to live differently?
- What do I need to do to live the life I want to live?
- What do I need to modify?
- What needs to happen?'
- Who do I need to become?

The questions I am sharing with you are the result of lots of study and personal work with my mentors and teachers, reading, introspection, awareness, and growth, but they can be great starting points for you.

For me it was all about coming to the realization that no matter where I went, what situation I had experienced in the past, what situation I was experiencing in this moment, or what situation I would experience in the future, there would always be ONE and only ONE constant, ME!

I take myself everywhere I go; I am the common denominator of all my experiences.

If I didn't change, really nothing else would change. The characters around me could change, the situation could change, the scenery could change, but the end result would be exactly the same because it was me who was involved in each one of those scenarios.

I invite you to make peace with whatever happened in the past, and keep moving forward. You cannot change the past any more than you can change what you had this morning for breakfast. You cannot control the future because it is not here yet. The only thing you can control is you. The only chance of even having the slightest possibility to control the future is to control the decisions you're making right here, right now, today in this moment.

What decision do you need to make today to ensure you will have a better tomorrow?

It is as simple (and yet as difficult) as that.

Beyond the Lies.

LET'S RECAP:

Stop blaming others. That is the key to your success. It is as simple as that, and as complicated as that. It's simple to say, but difficult to achieve without daily introspection, awareness, intention, and action.

If you want to change your situation, the one who has to change is you. The only thing you need to focus on iswhat you are feeling, what you want to change, and what you want to experience. You need to put all your energy into changing your situation first and foremost.

Find the ways to be happy and satisfied whether or not anyone around you changes ..

The journey is about you, not about anyone else, not about anything else, just YOU. What you need, what you want, what you desire, the way you want to live, the life you want to live, what I call "living life" is on your own terms.

Be strategic with your moves.

Life is a game, the most important game you will ever play, but a game nonetheless. The faster you realize this, the better equipped you will be to play to win.

Life is a game that cannot be lost, unless you give up. If you do, then the game is over, and that is a whole different story.

Never, ever, EVER give up!

I recommend you ask yourself the same questions I asked myself:

- If nothing else changes, if I assume no one around me will change, what do I need to do to live differently?
- What do I need to do to live the life I want to live?
- What do I need to modify?
- What needs to happen?
- Who is the person I need to become to realize my objectives?

CHAPTER FOUR
TAKE RESPONSIBILITY

**"The willingness to accept responsibility
for one's own life is the source from which
self-respect springs."**
- *Joan Didion*

Often times we look outside ourselves for answers to our problems. As human beings, we have a tendency to believe that our issues can be removed from us instead of knowing they are being held within us. We start by blaming the government or society, and then we get closer to home. We blame our parents and our closest loved ones. Closer still, we blame our significant other. However, the true cause of our malaise is our internal self.

You have to take responsibility; there is simply no other way around it. **Take responsibility for everything you say, everything you think, everything you feel, and every action and reaction you have.**

You need to ask yourself at any given moment: How am I responsible for what is going on right now?

Don't get me wrong. I am not implying that you should blame yourself, or feel guilty for your circumstances, because those two emotions are as disempowering and useless as external blame. What I mean is that you should ask yourself: What is my share of responsibility in these particular circumstances? How could I have showed up differently? How could I have entered the situation with a more positive intention?

Only when you take responsibility for your experience will you be able to take back your own power. The most common way in which people give away their power is by thinking that they don't have any. It is by accepting responsibility that you become empowered, that you are able to take back the power to change your circumstances for the better.

Your power cannot be stripped from you. If you feel you have lost it, then you need to reflect on the many ways you have actually given it away. I promise you if you look intently, you will be able to pin point when it was that YOU gave that power away.

The path to reclaiming that power starts with taking responsibility both for the ways you have given it away and by assuming the actions that will help you regain it.

There are very few things that will give you back your power as much as becoming financially independent, whatever that means for you. Maybe in your case it means starting that business you have wanted to start for so long, or growing the business you started a while ago, but have not been able to fully monetize. Perhaps it means directing your already successful business to the next level.

Whatever it is, the best way to become empowered is to become financially independent. When you are financially independent, you can truly be your own person and be unapologetic for who you are and living life on your own terms.

Sometimes becoming financially empowered is a long journey, especially when you have not been independent before or for quite some time. However, as with any change, there is always a first step.

My first step was at my therapist's office when she asked me: "Are you ready to do the work?" And I replied with an enthusiastic "Yes!"

She continued, "Are you willing to trust me through the process, even when it seems that we are getting nowhere because at times it will feel like that?"

Once again I said, "Yes!"

But inside, I felt a little less secure. I thought to myself: Now what? What is the next step? What is going to happen to me? What am I supposed to do next?

And then my therapist voiced my inner concerns. She

said,"Yes. I hear everything that you are going through, Erika, and how all the reactions of other people don't support what you would like to be experiencing. But I think that we should focus on you. We should start seeing how *you* have somehow ended up at the center of all this."

Well, that marked the beginning of my understanding of what taking responsibility meant. And now I know it means focusing on your own experience, and figuring out how you can take responsibility for whatever happened in your life to get you to where you are now, regardless of your external circumstances.

As simple as it seems, this acceptance is very difficult to achieve. It involves changing your way of thinking and reacting to the external circumstances that prevented you from achieving your goals and objectives. In these moments, you need to ask yourself:

What did I fail to recognize?
What did I fail to do?
What did I fail to become aware of?
What was I *not* willing to do?

Soul-searching is the way you will eventually realize why you did not achieve what you wanted to achieve, or why you are not experiencing what you wish you could experience. It is not easy, but it is the only effective way to ensure that we

Beyond the Lies.

learn from the situation we are currently going through.

It is only through that awareness and subsequent learning that you will be able to decide how you want to show up next time, the things you will modify, what decisions you will make differently, and how you will show up differently in that situation next time around. Going through this process is the only way in which change can start to take place.

Now here is the catch. It takes years of learning to see things in a certain way, and changing that perspective is not easy. You have to understand that you are battling against years of conditioning. However, with daily awareness, commitment and a strategy, your life perspective can be changed.

Let me give you an example. When you were very young, you saw a door in front of you, and you just didn't know how to open that door. You probably didn't know if it was just closed or locked, but regardless of this you knew you wanted to figure out how to open it.

Right now, many years later you know that you need to take certain actions to open that door. You can either turn the knob to the left or right, jiggle it up and down, or push or pull it. It's an automatic response. You don't have to think about the actions you will take anymore. Your approaches to opening the door are instinctive and imprinted in your cognitive memory. Through experience, you've taught yourself to react in ways that will solve your problem, i.e. open the door.

If you did not rely on your acquired knowledge and instinct, you would drive yourself crazy trying to think about how to perform the most mundane of tasks every single day, getting dressed and ready for work, as an example. However after many attempts, all these little daily tasks in your life are pretty much effortless.

Well, in that same way, our default tendencies take over when confronted with a situation, and they make us react pretty much automatically. It really requires great effort and time to change. The positive news is that when you actually do change, nothing is more rewarding.

When you are trying to make sense of what's happening in your life so you can actually decide how to respond differently, the default tendency is to start looking on the *outside*.

You say to yourself: What is happening *on the outside* that is making me experience what I'm experiencing at this moment? We believe that if we can only find the outside causes of what's happening to us, then we can come up with a solution.

Because we have been conditioned that way, we start to look outside rather than look within ourselves. We believe our

Beyond the Lies.

circumstances have to do with things as removed from us as, say, the economy, the government, our healthcare system, the owner of the company we work for, our partner, our children, our neighbor, or someone in our community.

Therefore, we're probably going to react to our problems by putting the blame elsewhere, by saying to ourselves something to the effect that "My life is like this because my friends did this to me, or other people I know did that." We may even go so far as to blame our parents or significant other. But the sad truth is that all those questions won't solve your problems.

As you start thinking more about your situation, hopefully you will start getting closer to the source of the problem you need to deal with. Finally you will realize that it is not about any of those people or circumstances surrounding you, but rather about how you are deciding to show up in each of these interactions.

At one point in time, I did not like many things in my life: the mother I was, the way my weight and health had been neglected, and the state of my marital relationship. I guess, in a sense, I did not like the woman I had become. It took a lot of courage and vulnerability to accept that fact, but once I did, I was able to see what I needed to change.

And actually, the change started in the following way.

Because I had been an athlete most of my life, I had always exercised. When I was in school, I did all sorts of activities. I did competitive swimming, played basketball and volleyball. After school, I took contemporary dance lessons, so I was always on the move.

I remember a time when I was around nine years old. My mom got home early from work. I'm kind of embarrassed to admit this, but I was watching a Mexican soap opera on television. I had been in front of the television for probably an hour or two by the time she got home, and she went ballistic.

My mom suddenly started screaming at me, telling me how bad it was to be in front of theTV for so long, and asking how could I possibly be watching a soap opera? What was I thinking?! She was very angry at the lady who took care of me for letting me watch that show, and she was even angry at my grandmother, who was living with us, for allowing me to watch that kind of program.

So she did what any empowered woman would do. My mom disregarded everything else and took matters into her own hands. The next day, she enrolled me in after-school activities that started from the time I left school until mid-afternoon. I barely had time for anything except to eat, do my homework, and go to sleep at night.

So that is how I grew up, with almost no TV. But it was a good thing, really, because this is why I turned to sports.

Beyond the Lies.

I learned to be on the move, and I loved it. I loved to feel my body in motion. I learned to be fit and strong, and those qualities became an essential part of my personality. They became a part of who I was.

Later when I entered my teenage years, I joined my first gym. It was a Gold's Gym, very popular at the time in Mexico. I used to go every day. It was part of my daily routine. I especially learned to love aerobics, and I did step and aerobics classes every day. I eventually became good friends with my aerobics teacher. And once again, exercise became an integral part of who I was.

Around the same time, at age twelve, I started horseback riding. Gosh, how I loved my horses! I woke up every single day of the week at six a.m. to be able to ride my horses before school. I ran back and forth from the horse arena to school all day long. I lived to study, ride my horses, and spend time with my boyfriend and friends. That was my life, and I loved it.

So as an adult, when my life began to fall apart, I decided to take the first step to change it. Since I was overweight and out of shape, the very first thing I did was get back into shape. I committed to getting myself into a "good" physical state. If I could not control anything else, I knew this was one part of my life that I could take control of. It was something I knew how to do, and it was easy and fast. I had results immediately.

I went to the gym at least three times a week, and I started to get into shape again, and in a sense reclaim my self-assurance and self-esteem.

I didn't want to use the excuse that I didn't have time to exercise because I had two very small children, or because my husband didn't want me to leave the family on the weekends, or simply because I was too tired because I was still breastfeeding. No, I knew that I had to take responsibility and make the change.

And that was the beginning of the physical change in my life.

Meanwhile, emotional changes were taking place as a result of work with my therapist. I had also committed to a process of personal growth, and made it a priority in my life.

Spiritually, I committed to learn how to meditate, to stay in silence, and listen to my intuition. I remembered how to pray, how to ask for guidance, and especially how to listen for the answers and be aware of them when they came.

I started my spiritual journey with simple things. For instance, I began asking for help with very small endeavors, like when I lost the car keys. I would ask the angels for help in finding those keys, and every time I would find them.

Beyond the Lies.

I even asked for help finding a parking spot in a crowded shopping mall, and every time, even to this day, I always find a parking spot near the entrance... and very fast! It never fails. My kids make fun of me. They say, "Mom, how do you do it? How do you make this happen every single time?" And my answer to them is always the same. "I just ask my angels; they always have a spot ready for me."

When you start asking for small stuff and you get answers every single time, this builds your confidence and your trust. And then you can start asking for guidance and help on bigger issues.

LET'S RECAP:

Step 1: Take responsibility.

Accept the responsibility. There is simply no other way around it. Take responsibility for everything you say, think, and feel, as well as every action and reaction you have.

The path to reclaiming your power starts with taking responsibility both for the ways in which you have given it away, and initiating the actions that will help you regain it.

You need to ask yourself, at any given moment:
- How am I responsible for what is going on right at this moment?
- What is my share of responsibility in this circumstance?
- How could I have shown up differently? How could I have entered the situation with a more positive intention?
- What is it that I failed to recognize?
- What is it that I failed to do?
- What is it that I've failed to become aware of?
- What is it that I was *not* willing to do?

Step 2: Make a commitment to yourself.

What am I going to be committed to?

What result or results do I want to experience in my life and business?

Step 3: Take Action.

What do I need to do *right away* to start the process of change?

What is the next step I need to take to get out of this rut?

Is there anything I need so I can take that action?

If the answer to any of the above questions is 'yes', then how can I make sure I respond right away?

CHAPTER FIVE
CHANGE ALWAYS STARTS WITHIN

**"I can't change the direction of the wind,
but I can adjust my sails
to always reach my destination."**
- *Jimmy Dean*

Nothing really happens until you realize that you have the power to decide how you are going to act in every single circumstance and at every single moment of your life, no matter what others do, or how others react.

It isn't until you are able to look at the core of your experience, until you're able to look at all those things around you as being the effects instead of the real cause of your circumstances, that you can begin to initiate any kind of change.

It is only when you're able to realize that it is your *internal self's* way of showing up in every single circumstance that you will understand the need to change that inner self in order to alter your outer circumstances.

Often I do an exercise with my clients where I ask them to close their eyes and think about a situation in which they were really happy about their circumstances;. I invite them to go back to a moment where everything was going well and they were happy, fulfilled, and in a positive state of mind. Then I ask them to describe that situation to me.

After that, I say to them, "Okay, now do the same exercise, and this time, think about a situation or a moment in your life where nothing was working, in which you were dissatisfied, angry, and even resentful. Describe a time when you felt you were in a hopeless situation. Now describe that situation for me. What was happening around you? What were you feeling? What was causing that circumstance?"

We would repeat the same exercise with each situation, and I would ask them to look for the characteristics that were similar in all of their experiences. Often there weren't too many similarities, but there was always a common factor, namely themselves.

No matter where you go or what you do, no matter what you are experiencing or who are you with, there is always only one commonality: yourself. You take yourself to wherever you decide to go.

So I invite you to do the same exercise:. Put yourself in whatever situation you're experiencing at this moment, a situation you're dissatisfied with or would like to change. Keep in mind, though, that in life it's impossible to change something external, and it's impossible to change anybody else. The only thing that you can do is start to take responsibility for your part in the story.

Beyond the Lies.

What do you need to change? Who do you need to be in the process, so the actual external circumstances change? What kind of thinking do you need to embrace to be able to change that circumstance? What kind of consciousness do you have to acquire?

What do you need to believe is possible to do or have so you can continue to take action? What is the belief system that you must have to propel you to take clear and consistent action?

To help you take responsibility for your circumstances, you need to ask yourself:

If it is true that I am responsible for what I am experiencing at the moment, what is my actual responsibility in this part of the story? How are my behavior, my thoughts or even my belief system getting in the way of my experiencing that which I truly wish to experience?

Let me ask you something. If all this is true, to what degree are you actually responsible for what's happening to you? What part of the responsibility can you accept?

Only when you understand this concept and finally take back your own power to change your circumstances, will you realize that it is the *change in yourself* that will make a difference in your reality. Only then will you start to feel in control of your life again. And until you embrace your inner knowledge and power, there will be nothing but insecurity, lack of control, and a perceived sense of being trapped in your circumstances without the possibility of change.

If you don't have the power to change those circumstances, if it is not within your reach, then the only way to change your circumstances will be by someone else's effort or external circumstances beyond your control. And that, of course, is a very disempowering feeling, and as we have discussed before, not even possible.

You must say to yourself: "Okay, wait a second. How can I actually think differently? How can I actually react differently? If it's true that I am responsible for what's happening, then what is my role, and how can I begin to arrive at a different awareness and perspective?"

In that moment of understanding, you will have gained *empowerment*, and there is nothing that will give you more freedom than that. It is only in that moment that you will truly be able to create lasting change in yourself and your life.

When I was going through this process myself, the first thing that I started doing was reflecting on the ways in which I had made decisions in the past. I said to myself, "Okay, if all this is true, then how did I actually end up living like I am living today? What decisions did I make at certain points in my life that got me to where I am today?"

If I return to that moment in which I was living a better life, when I was happier with my circumstances, when I was exhilarated about waking up every day and felt I was living my best life ever, I can ask myself:

- What has changed since then?
- What were the decisions that I have been making between then and now that got me to where I am today?
- What is it that I need to do *right now* to start making different decisions?
- What decisions do I need to stop making?
- How can I actually start making decisions based on the objectives that I have for my life?

I became acutely aware that if I was going to change my circumstances, I first had to become responsible for everything that happened in my life.

How that started for me is that I decided that I needed to become financially independent again. At that time I was living in Brazil. I must say Brazil is a wonderful country, full of great people. I was in a very beautiful area of town where my family and I were fortunate to be living in a gated community with a series of buildings which provided a common area where the children could play. I was living on the second floor of a building, and my windows opened onto a gorgeous oak tree with a spectacular view of greenery.

Although I was living in a lovely place, I felt isolated. My life consisted of taking care of my children, day in and day out. I couldn't work since I didn't have a work permit, and in my previous job interviews in other countries, they didn't want to give me the position because I was the wife of an expatriate. The employers knew that we would not be in the country for a long period of time, so they did not want to invest the time or money to hire someone only to see that person leave in a few years.

Experience had shown that it was not going to be easy to get a regular job at a company, so I naturally felt isolated, alone, and trapped.

On top of that, I had been out of the work force for over eight years, and I was clueless as to how to find a job that would provide me financial independence, while still being able to be present in my children's life.

The only people I had around me were the wives of other expatriates who were basically in the same situation that I was. Besides that, I knew that they were not going to be around for long either. It is difficult to build long-lasting relationships when you're relocating every couple of years.

Every relocation consisted not only of the loss of the relationships I already made in that country, but also the loss of the country which we had come to like and feel comfortable in, the places we were familiar with, and the shops we frequented.

Beyond the Lies.

As trivial as this may seem, I began to realize how such small details were the ones that brought us a sense of security and control over our environment and life itself. The need to find new places to live in a different country, the necessity of finding different schools for our children, as well as making new friends, learning different languages, and settling into new communities was exceptionally demanding.

If that was not enough we also had to learn to understand and adapt to the different social and cultural expectations of the people in the new countries in which we settled.

This is what would be considered a constant set of losses in one's life. With each one of those relocations, a part of your identity is stripped from you, and every time you get to these new countries, to these different situations, you have to start rebuilding an understanding of what your role will be in that environment. You have to adopt different routines and adjust to totally different ways of life.

I guess you've heard many times that you need to have a support group around you composed of family, friends, a job, associations, the places you like to frequent, and so on. Obviously when you're a mother that support group is an absolute necessity so that you can assist other members of your family in their adjustment.

When you relocate, that basic support system, including your family, the comfortable familiarity of routines that are part of your everyday life and experience, is stripped from you.

Every single one of these relocations means building a brand new support system from scratch. In a sense, each one of these relocations is a big loss you have to mourn. You have to make peace with the fact that your old, comfortable world is no longer present, and you have to forge a new life with new objectives.

When I was going through all these relocations, I became terribly depressed. I didn't feel useful because I didn't have a job or a community of friends and family to support me in those foreign environments. So I spent seemingly endless days just going through the motions, trying to make sense of all the emotions and situations that I was experiencing.

Trying to understand what I was feeling, what was happening around me, and trying to understand how I would rebuild my life again in this new country was exhausting. Yet I had to somehow summon the will, the strength and determination to meet new people and start all over. I had to put on a smile, be happy, and tell myself that I was looking forward to the experience.

Beyond the Lies.

My husband saw me in such a desperate state that he suggested I go to job interviews and ask people to hire me without pay at first. What I really needed, aside from the money, was to have something productive to do with my days - to feel useful that I was contributing in some way. I guess in a sense I was looking for what every human being wants and needs in this world which is experiencing a deep sense of significance and contribution. We all need to find a *why* to our lives beyond merely staying at home and waiting for our partner or loved one to return.

So that is exactly what I did. I remember going to work interviews and pleading with the people who would interview me. I'd say: "Please hire me. You don't even have to pay me." At that time, I didn't need the money as much as I needed the work for my sanity.

Unfortunately, potential employers wouldn't give me a job because they knew I was going to relocate again because I was the wife of an expatriate and would not remain in the country for a long time. For those reasons, they did not want to invest in my training and development, so many individuals replied, "I'm sorry, but I can't hire you because I want somebody for the long run."

Because of this, I concluded that in order to become financially independent, I would very likely not be working for someone else.

First, because I was relocating so often, and second, because I didn't want to be away from my children in a job that stretched from eight o' clock in the morning to eight o' clock at night. Doing so would mean being unable to be present for them, and just thinking about it broke my heart. One of my top priorities was to be there for my children.

At this time, I became acutely aware that the only way to fulfill my objectives would be to build my own business, and I knew that it had to be on my own terms. That is probably the first time I came to understand at a deep level what the expression "Living life on your own terms" meant. I didn't have an idea yet how to actually do it, but what I *did* know was that that was exactly what I wanted to experience. And I was also very aware of what I did *not* want to experience.

So the first thing I did was to start looking. I started a process of soul-searching – asking myself what it was that I needed to study and learn so that I could actually have my own business.

Now, even though I became aware at a conscious level that I needed to become financially independent and that I needed to stop waiting for other people to change, I still held this belief that something magical would happen and people around me would change. I had been like this for many years, without noticing, and old patterns are hard to break.

I was still trying to change my external circumstances

Beyond the Lies.

while I was going through the process of changing myself.

The process of changing yourself is not something that happens overnight even though you've arrived at an intellectual realization of what needs to happen. The actual process still takes quite some time to materialize.

While I was going through the inner transformation, I was still trying to make people around me change. But eventually, as often happens, I finally 'got it.' That day I was sitting with my mentor, and a light bulb flashed in my head. At that moment, I understood that the reason other people weren't changing was because they were fine as they were. In fact, it was me who had a problem! This intense realization or 'eureka' moment marked the before and after in my life.

The only one who had a problem in this story was me. The one who wanted to experience something different - more freedom or more happiness or different work or some other experience - was me. I was the one who needed to change!

And in theory, all that sounds really good, but putting it into practice is where the challenge truly begins. What I see happening is that many times when you embark on the process of personal transformation - and I know because it happened to me, and I have seen this with my clients too – you unconsciously not only want to change your circumstances, but you also hope that other people will do two things:

1) Be okay with what you're doing - in a way, give you permission, and tell you that you're doing the right thing; *and*

2) You wish they would change right along with you and see things the same way that you are starting to see them.

Most likely, these things won't happen because the one embarking on the journey is you. The one wanting to change is you, not them. Never forget that.

When others do not change their perspective, or when they don't approve of what you want to do, what will likely happen is that you'll get frustrated. You'll start doubting whether you are on the right path or not.

And that, my friends, is a deadly mistake. The sooner you understand that the only one who wants to change is you, and thus the responsibility to change is yours, nobody has to agree with what you want to do. Nobody has to embark on the journey with you. The sooner you come to realize this, truly accept it and move forward, the easier and faster you can wholeheartedly embrace your journey of change.

You shouldn't be waiting for somebody else to tell you "It's okay; go ahead. I support you," but instead you should be able to set out on your journey no matter what anybody else thinks or says, because you know in your heart that is what you need to do.

Beyond the Lies.

When I realized all this and when I embraced the fact that I needed to change, I committed to keep working with my mentor for at least a year. During this apprenticeship, we only focused on me - on my stories, my life circumstances, and what I wanted to do. For my part, this involved engaging in some soul-searching regarding what it was that I wanted for my future. That is when my life started to change.

What I see happening over and over again is that sometimes because you have not had a lot of experience actualizing your desires, you become accustomed to not even bothering to ask yourself what it is that you truly want. And of course, you don't feel secure enough to pursue it, even if you feel an urge inside. You bury your heart's desires, and by doing so, you begin to forget that they even exist.

If this is your case, I have a very straightforward solution to your problem. Every time you are unsure of your vision for your future, start to be very clear about what you *don't* want first. Sometimes the easiest way to find what we *do* want is to define in a clear way what we don't want. That is a very strong beginning.

Throughout the growth process with my mentor, I started going back to doing the things that I loved to do. One of the things that I did was to find things that would put me in a place of balance in four areas of my life. I wanted to achieve mental, emotional, physical and spiritual balance and alignment. That is the way in which I live my life every single day, striving for a way to align my activities, situations, and relationships with my mental, emotional, physical and spiritual objectives. I am always striving for experience, to continue a way of life that is in alignment with my values and vision of where I want to go in my life.

At that time, I began to pursue interests I'd suppressed. So I started to read for pleasure again, and looked for books I'd enjoy reading. In fact I read like crazy, finding topics I wanted to learn about. I became fascinated by all kinds of ideas that opened my mind to a completely new reality, to totally new possibilities as to how I could live my life and the principles that I could employ to change my experience.

As I started opening myself to different ways of thinking, my horizon of possibilities started expanding, too.

Whereas before it had felt like I was in a narrow dimly lit tunnel, which I could barely perceive the end of, suddenly I started to see the light showing me the way. And the more I continued reading and learning, the more that tunnel opened up to a wonderful new reality, revealing a fantastic new world I didn't even know existed.

What is interesting about this experience is that sometimes when we feel trapped in our circumstances, the reason we feel trapped is because we cannot see the exit. We cannot see the solution or perceive the possibility of change in our circumstances. However, rest assured that the only reason you don't see that possibility and you feel a sense of hopelessness is because of your perception of the situation.

Although that may be your reality right now, I want to communicate a profound sense of empathy and respect for whatever situation you may be living in this moment. More importantly, though, I want to reassure you that it is not the only truth.

I guarantee you that if you open yourself to possibilities; a new reality will come your way. You will see a better way of being and living that you didn't even know existed, where there is nothing but endless opportunities for growth, love and fulfillment.

And at this time, if you feel that you're inside a dark narrow tunnel, the only thing I ask is that you trust that your current reality is not the only available option in this universe. I ask you to trust that this universe is infinite with opportunities, and we are just a little grain of sand in a vast ocean of possibilities. Remember that there is always potential for a more fulfilling life. Your only job is to never, ever give up looking for it!

EMOTIONAL:

As I mentioned, what I did to restore my emotional alignment was to commit to working with my mentor for at least a year. I knew that there were no easy fixes, no simple solutions, and no magic pills. The only way through this process was to be open to inner change, to work hard, and to make a firm commitment to growth.

After that year was over, I became aware that I needed to continue the work I had started. That was over ten years ago, and I am still on the journey. Today, one of my main priorities is to make sure that I exercise my daily process of awareness, and work on a weekly basis with my mentors.

PHYSICAL:

I committed to doing a physical activity at least four times a week.

At that time in my life, I had gained more weight than I had ever gained before. In the process of opening up myself to my dreams and what I wanted to achieve in my life, I started to respect my physical needs and take care of myself. Therefore, I committed to following a proper diet and a regular exercise routine.

I made sure that every single day I did some sort of physical activity, even if it was only fifteen minutes of walking around my compound. Today, what I see happening is that many people don't exercise because they have this belief that exercise has to be strenuous and long-lasting, and that it has to be done in a location like a gym.

Beyond the Lies.

I am here to tell you that whatever kind of physical activity you decide to do, it's okay as long as you get your body moving. As I said, sometimes just a 15-minute walk around the block or a 45-minute run is enough. It's important to challenge yourself to go further each time, to push yourself out of your comfort zone. It's also important not to over-exert yourself and to follow your body's needs, or you'll end up being frustrated and giving up altogether. Work at your own pace and with your own schedule, but be committed to exercising and moving your body every single day . That's all that matters.

A body in motion stays in motion.

SPIRITUAL:

One of the major areas of your life is your spiritual side, the divinity inside of you that is in sync with the universe and with every living creature on the planet.

Sometimes we forget that we are just human beings, and it is impossible for us to achieve all we want to achieve on our own.

Besides that, if we focus only on ourselves, we have a lonely existence. It is when we're able to align ourselves with the universe around us - with a spirit, nature, a higher power, or when we embrace a personal concept of spirituality - that we feel a sense of connection and being grounded or present in our reality.

In my case, it started by committing to reading spiritual topics and doing at least five minutes of meditation a day. And when I mean meditation, what I started doing was just sitting on the floor with my back straight, focusing on my breathing, and keeping my mind relaxed for just five minutes. Five minutes of calm and silence can go a long way.

I have to tell you that when I committed to this routine, I started to become aware of so many more emotions I had, and I began to really become attuned to the subtleties of life around me. This ongoing meditation practice not only increased my sense of inner peace, but also heightened my overall awareness of life and myself. I began to articulate all the feelings that I had, but couldn't express before.

It's hard to believe, but just five minutes a day of silence and focused breathing can make a big difference in your life.

LET'S RECAP:

Nothing really happens until you realize you have the power to decide how you are going to act in every single circumstance and at every single moment of your life, no matter what others do, or how others react.

You are the center of your experience.

Your outer circumstances are the product of your inner thoughts. Who you are is the result of your belief systems, your degree of consciousness, and your life choices.

When you say: "Okay, wait a second. How can I actually think differently? How can I actually react differently? If it's true that I am responsible for what's happening, then what is my part in it, and how can I begin to arrive at a different awareness and perspective?"

In that moment of understanding, you will have gained something called *empowerment*, and there is nothing that will give you more freedom than that. It is in that empowerment that you will truly be able to begin creating lasting change in yourself and your life.

Understand that you are the only one who wants to change, and thus the responsibility to change is yours. Nobody has to agree with what you want to do. Nobody has to embark on the journey with you.

Find ways in which you can achieve balance in four areas of your life:

Physical
Emotional
Mental
Spiritual

What actions can you take starting today to achieve balance in those four areas?

Physical

_____

_____

Emotional

_____

_____

Beyond the Lies.

Mental

_____

_____

Spiritual

_____

_____

CHAPTER SIX
WHAT IS IT THAT <u>YOU</u> TRULY WANT?

**"We begin to die the moment we become
quiet to the things that matter."**
- *Nelson Mandela Jr.*

The process of soul-searching was a process of becoming acutely aware of everything around me - all my emotions, thoughts, and actions. When I was actually able to become aware of what I was thinking, feeling, and why I reacting the way I was in that moment, it was as if a little light had suddenly switched on inside of me – a small fire began to flicker that had been dormant for many years.

Probably for the first time in over eight years, I started to experience a burning desire to do something different, experience something different, to create a better life. I was beginning to feel alive again.

Honestly, it felt like I suddenly lit up inside, and those flames warmed me. I felt inspired and hopeful, something I hadn't felt in such a long time.

I felt like a child again. Children have dreams and wonderful imaginations. They are not afraid to speak their minds or say what they feel. They are not ashamed of their desires and regularly indulge in daydreaming. They are not afraid to tell you with excitement and hope what they wish to accomplish.

Unless someone has extinguished their bright flame, children feel emotionally alive most of the time. They are playful and rambunctious. They want to experience everything that is within their reach. They dance and run and move, and they want to do as much as they can every day, in every single moment. They are in their natural element, generally spontaneous and unaffected.

That daydreaming and natural exuberance help children be fully alive and experience a great sense of anticipation and hope for what lies ahead of them.

Children have all kinds of dreams. They want to become doctors, architects, veterinarians, artists, teachers, policeman, and the list goes on. Unfortunately, that burning desire is something, which often fades as you grow up. This happened to me.

The same way that a child dreams, you and I used to dream, too. Remember when we also had dreams, desires, and a great love for life?

Unfortunately, somewhere along the line, we lost or numbed those feelings of exuberance, anticipation, and desire to be alive. We even became ashamed of it because society made us grow up and abandon those feelings.

Beyond the Lies.

When we go to school, we are told that it's not okay to daydream. We are told we have to stay focused on facts. We have to be logical and memorize lots of facts, numbers, and information which turns out to be meaningless.

We are taught to recite history lessons by heart, and eventually we become memorizing machines (only to forget 80% or more of these facts as time goes by.) Unfortunately, the school system is not designed to help you become a calm, confident, compassionate, and aware human being. It is not designed to create empathetic human beings. It is, however, designed to create thinking, performing, work-oriented, and obedient machines.

Today's society is not focusing on creating happy and satisfied human beings, emotionally mature and compassionate human beings. Instead, it is turning out highly dissatisfied, fearful, and stressed individuals who feel that they are somehow flawed if they cannot keep up with others and with societal expectations.

Is it any wonder, then, that many individuals grow to adulthood not knowing what they truly want, only knowing what they are *supposed* to want, what society tells them is good for them? They know what is expected of them, but they often feel defeated by a sense of hopelessness or fear of not being able to meet those expectations.

With this imposed mindset, it's often impossible for

such individuals to make empowered decisions aligned with their true objectives. Somewhere along the line, as children, they lost the ability to trust themselves, and even acknowledge what they truly feel, think, and want. They have only been taught to memorize and regurgitate as opposed to relying on their own judgment as to what is meaningful to them.

Sadly, many of us often have to spend years, not to mention a countless amount of money, to repair our inner confidence and sense of inner strength which has been profoundly damaged during our formative years. This also impacts our self-esteem, capacity to dream, and instinctive sense of knowing what we truly want.

The truth is that we become indoctrinated. We begin to put more emphasis on what others want and need, rather than focusing on what we truly feel, think and need. By doing so, we eventually lose the capacity to trust our instincts, which society has repeatedly told us are wrong, or even shameful.

Too many of us have been taught to become silent to the things that truly matter. In that sense, our soul is damaged in a very fundamental way.

But since this is not a discourse on all the things that the educational system is lacking, I will stop my rant here.

I'd like to return to the importance of getting in touch with that burning flame inside of us which is called desire.

Beyond the Lies.

Rather than make us feel ashamed or strange, it is nevertheless the very GPS or *true north* that will help us find what is truly valuable to us in life.

Tell me, when was the last time you asked yourself:

What is it that I truly want?

If nothing else mattered, if I did not feel responsible for other people, if it wasn't because of money, if I wasn't concerned with what other people believed, then what would I want to be doing?

What would I like to experience?

In what ways would I really like to spend the days, weeks, or years of my life?

What are those things that I secretly fantasize about, yet tell no one about?

What are those things that I would truly like to experience if everything would go my way?

I believe those are great questions for which to find the answers.

Remember that those should be *your* answers, not mine or your partner's, not your parents', not your friends' - but yours.

When I reignited the flame, when I found these desires again, it was like being reborn. I became aware that there were so many things that I wanted to do, and there were so many ways in which I wanted to help the world.

I realized that there were so many things that were happening in the world and in my life that were not okay. There were things that needed to change. I was not okay with the status quo, and the only way to change that was to transform my own life and myself.

Let me tell you, it felt really good to do that. It felt good because before embarking on my journey, I felt empty, and now, suddenly I was alive again. I had no idea how to achieve anything or even where to start, but at least I knew what I wanted. The first thing that I can remember is that I committed to the process of transformation.

To this day, one of the things that bothers me are the subliminal messages women receive suggesting they should just sit back and wait for someone to rescue them. Society, our families, schools, the media – still indirectly promote the idea that as women, all we need to do is worry about finding a man who will 'save' you, and your life will turn out just fine.

The message is that whatever situation you are experiencing, whether it is financial or emotional, all your

106

problems will be solved the day you get married. The assumption is that our mate will "complete you", so it follows that if you can find a man with means or prospects, then he will take care of you for the rest of your life. You will be safe and worry-free.

What lies we have bought into! That is the beginning of all the problems in society, and for women in particular. As women, we often approach our relationships from a perspective of being incomplete in ourselves, and needing someone to complete us, someone to protect us and rescue us of only God knows what… if you think about it, most likely rescue us from life….

We therefore search for that perfect counterpart who can provide what we somehow have been taught that we 'lack'. Is it any wonder, then, that the divorce rate is 50% for first marriages, 65% for second, and 72% for third-time marriages?

Most women learn to use their femininity and looks in exchange for security and financial stability from a partner, only to realize years later that that was exactly the beginning of all of their their problems. They are operating from a belief system that says they cannot have the life they desire on their own, that they are not capable of carving out their place in the world.

In that exact moment when you believe you have found the prince who's going to save you, you give your life away.

You are in danger because you are putting your life in someone else's hands.

I know that this is true because that is exactly what I did. I put my life in someone else's hands. In my case, it was because of the constant relocations, but even if it is by choice, the truth is that it does not matter in the end. My life was not my own. I made choices, and I had to take responsibility for what I had experienced as a result of those choices.

I experienced many years of relocating around the world with my family, living among the expatriate communities, among women who were in the same situation I was. And I can truly tell you that in eight years, I never found one woman who was completely happy and fulfilled. These were women who did not have a space of their own, but only waited for their partners to return from work and resume family life and responsibilities.

Were there women who had made peace with it? Yes, I believe so. Were there women who had learned to deal with it? Yes, once again. But I never found one woman who was truly fulfilling her purpose and expressing herself and her gifts, who was truly alive and feeling that she was making a difference in the world.

I was looking at everything around me and I remember thinking, "I don't want to live like this. I don't want to become one of these women. I don't want to spend the rest of my life like this."

So I began that process of soul-searching and reflection. Everywhere I went, I thought to myself, "This is not acceptable. We cannot continue to tell our daughters that this kind of restricted life is acceptable. We cannot continue to tell future generations that it is all right to look for somebody else to take care of you. That has to change, and I have to do my part to change that because my daughter is not going to grow up with those messages."

At this time, when I realized that I felt so passionate about the subject of women's freedom, it became really apparent to me that part of my journey had to be to find a way to not only empower myself, but also to empower the women of the world to change their stories, their lives, and particularly their financial situations. I needed to help those women get in charge of every aspect of their lives.

One last point before we conclude this chapter:

The life you're living today is telling a story. You are either telling a story of freedom and possibility, growth and life, or you're telling a story of sadness, conforming, or disempowerment.

What is the story your life is telling the world so far?

What is the legacy you will leave to the world when

your time on this earth comes to an end?

What kind of legacy do you want to leave?

Is the way you are living your life telling the story and leaving the legacy you want to leave?

LET'S RECAP:

Some great questions to ask yourself are:

What is it that I truly want?

If nothing else mattered, if I did not feel responsible for other people, if it wasn't because of money, if I wasn't concerned with what other people believed, what would I want to be doing?

What would I like to experience?

In what way would I really like to spend the days, weeks, or years of my life?

What are those things that I secretly fantasize about and that I tell no one?

What are those things that I would truly like to experience if

---

everything would go my way?

I believe those are great questions to find the answers to.

However, remember that they are *your* answers, not mine or your partner's, your parents', or your friends' - but yours.

When your life comes to an end, it is only you who will have known if you lived the life you wanted to live, or whether you were too afraid to go after what you truly desired.

The Choice is Yours.

CHAPTER SEVEN
THE SELFISH BITCH

"When you have a gift you do have to become fairly selfish. You cannot afford to let too many outside things get in the way."
- Sarah Brightman

The idea of the "selfish bitch" came about when I was growing up and feeling lonely. I also felt that my needs were not being made a priority. I'm sure that I was seeing things from the eyes of a youngster who did not understand the adult world, but at times I felt like everybody else was selfish, was taking care of their own wants and needs without thinking about mine. That was not a conscious thought. It was rather an omnipresent feeling that I had as a little girl. Nevertheless it took me many years to realize that that was my perceived situation rather than the truth of what was going on around me.

When we are little kids, it is very difficult to discern between our perceived reality and the understanding of what is truly happening. So what ultimately happens is that our perceived reality becomes our only truth, our only reality, and so it was for me. That was my truth, what I was feeling in my every day life.

What eventually happened was when I was in my 30s,

wanting to start a business and become financially independent, I didn't know how to do it. I was so afraid I would hurt my kids, or someone else would get mad at me. At the beginning it was difficult to move forward.

I noticed that as I was going through my own personal work and my own personal journey of starting and growing that business, one of the biggest challenges I had to deal with was my fear of being a selfish bitch.

For instance, I was afraid of being selfish by taking time away from my family to pursue my own interests. Initially, in fact, I almost stopped going after my dreams because of that fear and because I was feeling guilty for making myself a priority.

Everything I wanted to do felt selfish, even the study that I wanted to embark upon felt selfish. Every hour away from home felt selfish. Every penny I was thinking of using for my own studies felt selfish. I mean, at the very beginning, when I started exercising and working on my emotional needs, everything I did for myself felt selfish.

I eventually came to understand the underlying fear I had of being called a "selfish bitch" by others who stood in judgment of what I wanted, of who I was or of who I wanted to become.

That is one of the major issues that all women deal with

in one way or another. All of my clients have to deal with this guilty feeling at some point in their lives - especially when they have children and a family. This is an issue every woman deals with, especially when she is a mother.

Truth being told, women are used to endless giving, endless providing, and to making everyone else's needs and wants a priority before their own.

The truth is we want to see our loved ones happy. I know you want to see your children and your partner happy. It makes you happy, so you sacrifice and sacrifice, and sacrifice some more, until one day you wake up and feel empty inside. You have nothing left to give. In that moment you start to feel resentment and anger. The worst is yet to come. In that moment you start to feel awful and start to even hate yourself for having those feelings in the first place. In that moment all that anger and lack of happiness is turned inwards, causing more illnesses, more divorces, and more depression than society has ever cared to admit.

Unfortunately, because of that you may stop doing the things you love. You put your own dreams on the back burner. You say to yourself, "When the kids grow up...," "When _____ (your husband) has a better job...," "When we have more money...." Time passes... and passes...and it goes away.

For a woman, it is far easier to let herself down than to "hurt" those she loves the most. It is easier to hurt yourself than those around you. The eternal self-sacrifice of a woman, that notion our grandmothers had passed on from generation to generation, grows without us ever intending for it to do so.

All this is a fertile ground for disillusionment, sadness, and a sense of not having a world of your own. You become part of everyone else's world, but you do not have one for yourself. You become "the mother of _____," "The wife of _____," "The daughter of _____," and you? Who are you? Where is that woman you once were?

The self-sacrifice, which at first feels like the right thing to do, may even make you feel proud of yourself. "I am being a great mom,. You may say to yourself, "This is what being a great wife means." That eventually starts to eat away at you. You may even become dissatisfied and depressed.

Any thought you may have had of doing anything for yourself brings up a little critical voice inside which pipes up, "I can't do that because that is so selfish." With time it becomes increasingly harder to suppress that voice, even though you know deep inside that you are lying to your true self and identity.

I believe the concept of being selfish or feeling guilty about wanting to go for what you want has been present in my life on numerous occasions. The only difference between then and now is that right now I can recognize that feeling more

116

easily, and therefore make different, more self-supporting decisions.

I do remember, though, the first time this feeling occurred. The first time was when my kids were really little (one and three years old). We were living abroad at the time, and I had breast-fed them both for a year each. That is when I came to understand the importance of getting some 'me time', the importance of doing activities that would nourish my body, mind and soul.

The breastfeeding, although fulfilling and life enhancing to them, was exhausting for me. It was physically exhausting and emotionally exhausting, too, particularly because my daughter constantly woke up through the night, wanting to be fed. Honestly, I was exhausted to the point of feeling like a zombie.- You know, one of those periods in your life where you just put one foot in front of the other and feel like you can't go on.

But I just didn't have time to entertain that feeling. I had two very small children to care for and all sorts of things going on in my life. I had gained a lot of weight. I wasn't exercising. I wasn't engaging in any kind of spiritual practice, and I wasn't reading a lot. I was just going through the motions trying to survive that very tumultuous period of my life.

The truth is motherhood is one of the most rewarding experiences a woman can have. Unfortunately it is also one of the most demanding and overwhelming experiences at the same time.

When I finally was very close to the end of my rope and I began to recognize I could not live like that, it was not supportive of my kids, let alone of me. One of the first things I did was to ask myself, "When was the last time you felt truly happy and alive in your life?"

The answer was apparent and always the same. It was when I was exercising - no matter what kind of exercise that was. The common denominator in all those times was when I was exercising and doing outdoor activity. I was always a person who enjoyed and craved physical activity.

At that time, however, I wasn't doing anything, so I decided to commit to working out in some manner for half an hour, at least three times a week. That meant that when I was not able to fulfill that commitment during the week I chose to exercise on the weekends.

Now that was my first challenge because the weekends were reserved for family routines and our quality time together. I had to actually leave my home and leave the children with my husband to go and exercise. Even though I knew it was beneficial for me, I still saw the act as selfish. It was an indulgence that appeared, at first glance, to be only for my benefit.

Beyond the Lies.

Naturally, it was hard to go against what other people believed I should be doing, but I must report I persevered anyways. I would get out of the house and go for a walk around my neighborhood - sometimes even do a run. I found ways in which I could exercise without having to take three or four hours from my weekend to do it. And you know what? It felt really good, and I started noticing that my positive energy had an impact on everyone else around me as well. Not only was I in a better mood, but I had more energy and felt proud of myself and what I was doing. I even began to feel more hopeful about my life in general.

I believe that this so-called feeling of selfishness is something that shows up for women at different stages in their lives, especially each time they're trying to improve themselves in one way or another.

Another occasion I can think of when this happened was when I decided to pursue a bachelor's degree in energy healing science. I decided to enroll in a four-year program to pursue one of my main passions in life, energy healing - the understanding of the human consciousness and spirituality.

This program required me to be away from home five times a year. That meant being away every two months for 10 days in a row.

As I mentioned, my children were very young at the time (two and four years old, respectively), and so the program called for a big commitment of financial resources, which I had not had to summon up since I graduated from college, and of my time and energy It was a commitment by my family to allow me that space, and it was a great deal of soul-searching on my part as to my true desires and intentions.

In this case, it was not merely a walk around the block, but it involved a greater commitment to being a student. This endeavor also involved travelling because I had to travel to another country to attend the school. I also had to lay out money for the airfare, hotel accommodations, meals, etc. However, the worst thing for me was that I had to be away from my young children for ten days in a row.

Once I made up my mind, however, I just knew that I had to stick with my plan. So I summoned all the strength that I could and said to myself, "This is what I need to do because otherwise a part of me will continue to die. I know this is my next step in my growth process, in my journey, and I need to do it no matter what. I need to be committed to what I want to do."

So I got on the plane that first time, and it was so difficult. I can still vividly recall how I felt that first morning when I opened the door to the house with all of my luggage, ready to embark on a trip, and for the first time leaving my kids behind.

Beyond the Lies.

How heavily that feeling of guilt and abandonment weighed on my shoulders. I felt awful. My heart was aching, and I was afraid. It was very difficult to leave the house. I remember how much I sobbed because I didn't want to leave my children. "What if they need me," I was thinking. "What if they get sick? What if they feel alone and scared, and Mom is not there?" I literally had to summon all my will and commitment to myself to leave the house and make that trip.

When I arrived at the hotel, I continued to cry I cried almost every night that I was there, with that nagging guilty feeling following everywhere I went. I saw other women who were in the same circumstance that I was, going through something very similar to me and feeling very similar feelings to those I was having.

I believe the best way I can describe it is by saying that I had an internal conflict happening inside. I felt guilty, sad and scared for leaving them for the first time. Yet I was thrilled about the journey I was embarking on, thrilled about what I was doing.

I knew I really wanted to be where I was, and I was going to be studying what I really loved. Nevertheless on the other hand, I missed my children and was so afraid that something would happen to them during my absence.

That was a very difficult time in my life, feeling so conflicted. The thing is that conflict was happening inside me, in my thoughts, in my feelings, and it was affecting my whole being.

This continued happening at least three of the five times I had to travel during the first year of the program. The curious thing about it was that each time that I would leave, my children would get sick.

My children were very healthy children. They would very rarely get sick. But this scenario would never fail: the day before I was to leave on a trip or the day after I left, the two of them would inevitably become ill, developing fevers, vomiting, and having to be removed from school.

On one of these educational leaves, when I was again sobbing in a school corridor, a dear friend of mine who came with me suddenly started crying along with me. We both said out loud, "What's going on here? What's happening?" My friend continued, "Every time I leave, my children get sick." I agreed with her, adding, "Well, mine are getting sick, too."

You know how in this universe there are no coincidences? Well, one of our teachers – who, by the way, was a male teacher - happened to be walking by at that moment. When he spotted us in tears, he asked, "What's going on?" We told him what was occurring, and he smiled at us in a very understanding way. Then he said, "Come with me, and I'll tell you a story."

Beyond the Lies.

We went with him to the cafeteria, and we all sat down together. He proceeded to tell us his story. He had gone to the same school as we (in order to teach there, you had to study there), and when he was going through his own training, each time he would leave his home, his children would become ill, too!

He explained to us how it was a transfer of energy. It was our own sense of guilt and stress as mothers, our own sense of abandoning our children, that was causing all the problems because that is what we were passing on to them.

Since we could not even understand this until it was explained to us, how could we expect our children to understand? Because they could not understand this in rational terms, they would instinctively react by developing symptoms of illness.

Then our teacher said, "Let's do an exercise," and he walked us through the importance of what we were doing for ourselves and how it wasn't selfish at all. He spoke of how it was actually benefitting our children He spoke with feeling and conviction, giving us a sound rationale as to why we were doing the right thing.

In that school, we had to have sessions with a counselor in between school weeks, and he said, "I want you to work from this school week to the next with your counselor on the guilt and confusion you feel when you leave your children so that you can get rid of that feeling. Then you'll be able to come to school with a sense of peace and happiness because you'll know that you're going to be a better person and that your children will therefore become better human beings in the process."

I swear to God, when we did that everything changed. I released the guilt and the feeling of being selfish, and my kids never got sick again. The same thing happened with my friend. I returned home after that talk, and even though they were young, I sat down, and we had a conversation.

I explained to them how much Mommy loved going to school, how important it was for me to go to school, all the things I was learning and doing, and how I was growing. I told them just how much I was looking forward to them coming to my graduation the first year so they could meet my new friends.

By doing this, I made them part of my world. I informed them that I would be away only a few days, and then I would return. I assured them that everything would be just fine and that they would be well taken care of. And interestingly enough, after that, they never got sick again. I was appalled to see how their sickness was a 'symptom' of my own anguish, my own projection of abandonment, and my fear that they would be hurt or even scared by my absence.

Beyond the Lies.

Now I believe every woman goes through a stage in which she is apprehensive, and of course you need to make sure that if you're going to leave your children for any period of time, they will be well taken care of. I'm not simply saying that you should leave your children without preparing beforehand, but once you make sure that they are going to be okay, that they're going to be loved and feel secure, then you really need to release your own feelings of selfishness, guilt or abandonment. If you do not, I believe you are actually hurting them more than you are helping them.

Of course I did work with my counselor on that specific issue (week three to four of Year One), but I also continued to do so throughout the years that I attended school. I continue that work even today as I am writing this book. The truth is that work is never over. You always get an awareness of a new layer that is revealed as you get to know yourself and your psyche better.

I must admit that today – many years since that first day of school – the issue of feeling guilty at times still comes up

As I said at the beginning of the chapter, it still arises, and I sometimes have feelings of guilt. I'll ask myself, "Is this the right thing? Am I abandoning the children? Am I doing the best thing for them?" However, because I've been working through this issue for such a long time, it's easier to understand what's going on and deal with it. I have come to accept that the feelings of fear and doubt will arise every time I choose to grow, to improve my life in some way.

What you need to do then is to work through it. Don't ignore those feelings or downplay them. Work through your issues, and make sure that you do so with either a coach, a therapist, a counselor, or a mentor. Choose your modality. I would just like to urge you not to sink in unawareness. You have to do that in order to be able to move forward in your life. In truth, *you need to know that you cannot give your children what you don't have yourself.*

You have to become the best version of yourself possible so that you can help your children and other people around you become the best version of themselves possible.

Will everything in your life be perfect? No, of course not.

Will your life be all pink roses and fairytales? Of course not. We are talking about life, not about some far distant reality that only exists in our imagination.

But you need to show up every day. You need to show up to the best of your ability as an aware purposeful person who is living her chosen life. You need to overcome your fears and doubts because, believe me, they will be present as you move forward, as you evolve, as you grow. You have to do the work; you can't just wait for them to disappear on their own. *You need to make a commitment to moving forward in your life - no matter what.*

Beyond the Lies.

I came to understand that Selfishness is not living the life you want to live. Selfishness is pretending others to live the life you want to live. *Go ahead and live your life on your own terms, and set others free to do the same.*

I would like to add one thing before we finish this chapter and that is that at the very beginning of any journey, you have desire – the desire to change or the desire to do or experience something different. But you often have fear as well, about how you will achieve this change and how it will turn out. You will have fear about the possibility of making more money or achieving whatever it is that you are pursuing in your business or life. And it is that insecurity, that lack of physical evidence, that sparks doubt in human beings.

That is what makes you feel guilty or selfish because you don't have concrete results yet. I want to emphasize the word 'yet' because success will come. When you take steps to enhance your business or your life, it's a proportional equation. When you take certain actions, you will achieve certain results. It's the law of cause and effect. You cannot expect to get the effect without the cause, but if you are the catalyst, you will certainly get the results you desire.

However, a word of caution. Those results take time, and while you are in the process of getting the results, you need to keep your faith. I heard someone say once that what keeps the human spirit alive is Faith, and Faith is believing in what you cannot see. Faith is believing despite not being able to "see" the physical manifestation of that thing.

It is the same with Trust. If you tell me that you will trust when you "see" something that is not trust. That is just being present in your reality. Your ability to trust starts the moment you remain certain about a fact whether you are able to "see it" or not.

You need to keep your spirit up, knowing and having confidence in what you're doing and in what you want to create. You must keep moving forward while those results start appearing in your life or business. You MUST keep moving forward, knowing, expecting that those results will come, because the truth is those results will be the effect of the real cause, which is you and your actions

LET'S RECAP:

I believe that this so-called feeling of selfishness is something that shows up for women at different stages in their lives - especially each time they're trying to improve themselves in one way or another.

Make peace with your family, your children or whoever you are separating from, or you may feel guilty for leaving behind part of your own experience. Share with them why this is so important to you. Assure them that everything will be just fine, that they will be well, and that you will come back.

Don't ignore those feelings or downplay them. Work through those feelings with a mentor, and do not sink in unawareness.

Selfishness is not living the life you want to live. Selfishness is pretending others to live the life you want to live. *Go ahead and live your life on your own terms, and set others free to do the same.*

You need to make a commitment to moving forward in your life - no matter what.

If you are feeling guilty ask yourself:

1) Is this feeling I am having about that other person(s), or about me? (My guess is the latter one.)

2) If I allow myself to live my life based on what I want to experience, will I "become more, grow more, and thus be able to give more to my loved ones?

3) How can I keep my faith up on the results I am trying to accomplish? How can I boost my motivation and expect the results will come in due time?

Guilt is one of the most unproductive emotions, acknowledge it, and move forward based on your objectives and the destination you see or wish for yourself!

CHAPTER EIGHT
PERMISSION TO SHINE – DECISION TIME

"In any moment of decision, the best thing you can do is the right thing. The worst thing you can do is nothing."
- Theodore Roosevelt

There is a moment in everyone's life when they have to make a decision, when they have to decide whether they are going to change their circumstances or just keep living the same reality.

Your moment of decision is when you ask yourself if you're going to keep complaining about not having what you really want which is to experience what you truly desire, or if you're actually going to make a decision to change, if you are going to actually do something about it, beyond complaining and feeling sorry for yourself.

When I say "moment of decision," it's because there is a moment in every person's life where you get to the edge of the cliff and going forward feels like a great leap of faith. You don't know what lies ahead because you don't have any experience in that realm. So at that moment, you have the choice to retreat to what you perceive is a safe place, even though you don't like it anymore, or take the leap even though you are afraid.

If what you said you wanted is really important to you, when you get to that moment of decision you need to be able to make what I call an unequivocal decision to change. Meaning you must acknowledge and say, "This is what I want. This is my next step, and I am going to take action no matter what happens next."

You may think to yourself, "I may not be able to see the entire path yet, but I do know that this is the next step. I will release any kind of worry or fear I have. I will put my sole focus and energy into making this next decision work for me."

Because the journey of a thousand miles, begins with the first step.

It is important to acknowledge that in that moment, if you don't move forward but instead retreat, you're just perpetuating your own patterns, the cycle of dysfunction, the patterns you have built for years and years, which have gotten you to where you are today.

Do not be mistaken. Do not believe that nothing will happen if you retreat. You have once again given yourself the experience of fear. You have added to the story of "It cannot be done. I cannot do it," and you continue to perpetuate the same cycles.

Beyond the Lies.

Unfortunately as women, we often find love, appreciation, and companionship in complaining. What that means is that it's not rare to see a group of women get together to complain and tell each other how miserable or how sad they are with the circumstances in which they are living. And yet, when the moment comes for them to make a change, when the moment comes to take action, they get afraid to make a decision, and they do nothing about their circumstances.

As I said in previous chapters, that decision may involve hiring a mentor or spending 30 minutes every morning to exercise because that's a non-negotiable. That decision may mean going back to school, or starting your business. It may involve getting the funding you need to start a business or even to hire the mentor who'll tell you how to do it. Whatever the decision is, you need to make it now and stop complaining. At a certain point, it's simply unproductive.

The problem is women often find attention and companionship in complaining. When we complain because we are hurt, sad or lonely, everybody comes to our rescue - our moms, our friends, whatever circle we live in. They embrace us; they love us; and inevitably they try to help us. The person who gives ears, attention and love to the complaining of others unfortunately becomes part of the problem instead of being part of the solution.

Unfortunately, we've made a value system out of struggling, and thus we're perpetuating the cycle of struggle within the feminine archetype. Women can feel comfortable in the "space" of struggle, in the "space" of complaining, in the "space" of rehearsing the story as to why they can not change their circumstances.

But let me ask you: What do you believe happens when a woman is successful? What happens when a woman is beautiful, successful, wealthy, and is traveling the world and living the life she wants to live?

Well, let me tell you what happens when a woman thrives. What happens is that the women around her start to criticize and attack her. God forbid you should walk into a room exuding happiness and tell everybody about your good fortune in life!

If you were a man, everybody would applaud, but because you're a woman, what is more likely to happen is that everyone, especially other women, start to criticize you. "Who does she think she is?" they say or think. "I wonder what she had to do to get that promotion," they say to themselves. Very often we live in a world of envy and criticism in which we feel compelled to criticize other people, as if we can find something that is wrong with them. That would mean that we are ok, that we are not wrong.

Beyond the Lies.

It is this incessant need to compare ourselves to something or someone else. But we need to stop comparing. We all have different lives, different circumstances and life experiences. We all have different backgrounds and different situations we go through.

When we criticize, it is because we are holding the idea that it's not okay to shine.

So many women are terrified to shine because they know they will be criticized. But you know what? It's time to stop asking for permission to shine. Give yourself permission to shine instead. When you give yourself permission to be as big, as vivacious, as exuberant, as happy, as alive as you want to be, in that moment you are empowering all the women around you to do the same.

You're empowering your children to do the same. You are empowering the world to do the same. And as a result, we start creating this value system around success, happiness, and positive things rather than around merely surviving, being sad, playing the victim, and struggling through life.

I know exactly how it feels to be criticized by the people around you, by the women around you. I experienced this first hand at a very young age.

I guess it started well before I was born. When my mother was growing up, one of her deepest wounds was that her family did not have enough money for her to dress nicely. She was always going to family events and social functions, and she was always self-conscious about what she was going to wear and the clothes she had.

So when I came along, and after she divorced my father, one of the things she really enjoyed was taking me shopping and buying me beautiful clothes - not necessarily expensive ones, but beautiful clothes. She always made sure I was well-dressed. This was important to her because of her own experience.

I remember going to department stores on the lookout for a shirt or a dress, and while I was in the dressing room, my mom would keep bringing clothes and more clothes for me to try. She would spend hours looking at me changing clothes and loved to buy me as many clothes as possible. I learned at a very young age the pleasure of trying new clothes and being dressed beautifully. I never understood there was something wrong in it, much less that being dressed in a certain way was something to be ashamed of.

But then when I was around twelve years old, my life made a big turnaround. Before that time I was quite popular at school. I had many friends, and we were all part of one big group. We were all friends. We embraced everyone in our grade. Everyone was invited to the gatherings and birthday parties. No one was ever excluded.

Beyond the Lies.

We were all very good friends, and we went in groups basically everywhere we went.

As I continued towards the end of seventh grade, it was more common than before to host parties at different of our friends' homes.

Quite a few of our friends in our grade were musicians, and they formed a band. So once in a while we went to concerts they would give. They were just simple, teenage concerts – no alcohol, as we were minors. There were always parents present, and it was a "clean" and "non-threatening" environment.

My mother had showed me how to dress up for special occasions. She would make sure that I was well put together. It was her special guilty pleasure, if you will.

But apparently other kids did not see this as a positive thing. I started to be criticized by other girls. They would look at me and would actually say, "Who do you think you are to be dressed like that? Why are you dressed like that?" adding "You're making me feel bad."

Little by little I started losing friends. These girls did not want to spend time with me because they felt threatened by the clothes I was wearing (Seriously? Well at that time it was not even funny. I did not understand why all of this was happening.) Most girls ended up being resentful, and I eventually ended up with only a handful of friends.

Let me tell you, having my own friends turn against me was a really painful experience. They were not strangers or boys, but girls with whom I'd formed bonds of trust, intimacy and friendship.

I believe this was the first time I experienced being "punished" by doing something I enjoyed, by standing out and being myself. It was the first time I learned first hand how scary it can be to stand out instead of blending in.

The worst thing was that the process was really painful. Without me noticing, I started tuning down, not only the way I dressed, but how much I expressed myself, how much I let my voice and opinions come through. Basically I started blending in for fear of standing out.

The worst part is that my female friends inflicted this pain. I was way too young to know how to deal with this rejection and with this situation. The only thing I knew to do was to stay quiet, blend in, and not "rock the boat" too much.

Why am I telling you this? Because I would love for you to recognize that, as women, we are all exactly the same. We have all loved, been betrayed, experienced pain. Many of us have been mothers. We have laughed, fallen on our faces, and then gotten back up again. If you're a mother, then you have experienced the love and pain of motherhood, too. If you have been in love, then you have at some time been deceived or hurt the same as I have. We all experience the same things.

Well, it is time for women to change this paradigm of criticizing, complaining and attacking other women. I think it is about time for women to stop putting other women down and instead join forces to form a powerful alliance that will enhance each other's life.

We have to find ways to feel special, loved and secure without the need to put someone else down, especially another woman.

A woman should be able to be as exuberant, as loud, as alive and as happy as she wants to be. We need to empower women to shine, and we need to create a value system based on celebrating the light within us.

You see, all women go through basically the same experiences. We love; we fall down; we are deceived. We stand up again, bear kids, laugh, and feel afraid. Those feelings, and more, are universal to every single woman.

The next time you see a woman, I invite you to look beyond her clothes, to see beyond the makeup she wears, beyond the handbag she carries, or how beautiful she looks on the outside. You never know what her inner reality is, what her fears are, what her pains are, what it is that she is truly experiencing.

I invite you to look at the woman herself - the sum of her pain, her joys, and her fears.

On a biological level, we are all the same, and we need to consciously create a better place where we are present for other women to help them shine and succeed in the world.

If what you want is to feel special and loved, please realize that there are ONLY two ways you can achieve this:
1) You can do something extraordinary yourself, or
2) You can go about it the wrong way and criticize other women in the hopes that this will help you feel better about yourself.

I certainly hope you choose the first option. The second one, no matter how long you do it, will always leave you with a sense of insecurity, emptiness, and anger; and what is worse, it is not even a sustainable way to feel good about yourself.

Please remember, if you're feeling the need to criticize another person, you're most likely not giving yourself permission to realize your own dreams. You are trying to get a positive feeling (happiness, fulfillment and significance) by "tapping" into the negativity of life (competition, lack, attack, anger and criticism). You can never every get something positive while spreading negativity around.

Beyond the Lies.

Don't you believe that the world would be such a different place if we could finally create an energy, a sisterhood, a consciousness of women being present and standing up for other women, instead of putting others down?

Wouldn't it be great to see women present to lift women up and give other women permission to shine, too?

I am here to state emphatically that every single person who criticizes another is not giving themselves permission to be, do, or have whatever it is that they truly desire.

If you're reading this book, then you're already in the process of doing something extraordinary with your life. You've already made a decision to leave all that negativity behind. Please, today take the next step.

Here's the thing. In life, there are only two ways to be significant. You either do something extraordinary yourself, or you criticize another human being because that sets you apart.

I certainly hope that if you're reading this book you belong to the first group, the accomplished group who gives themselves permission to shine and commit to doing something extraordinary on their own, the group who does not feel the need to put anyone down to accomplish what they need or want.

I certainly hope you want to belong to the group of women who is determined and committed to motivate and empower others to become the best version of themselves.

It is my desire that you become the person who is so secure and grounded in your own success and achievements that you do not feel the need to criticize others in order to feel significant yourself.

I especially hope, if you are a woman, that you commit to enhance the lives of other women. You commit to never put another woman down again, whether she is your daughter, your sister, your mother, your friend, or simply your acquaintance.

I invite you to know, and reflect on, that we are all the same. We are made the same; we experience and feel the same. We cry the same; we hurt the same. Have empathy for people. Do not put other people down.

I can assure you that if you do so, you will, by example and teaching, allow other people to embrace their greatness, too.

Beyond the Lies.

LET'S RECAP:

There is a moment in everyone's life when we have to make a decision, when we have to decide whether we are going to change our circumstances or just keep living the same reality.

When you get to that moment of decision, you need to be able to make an unequivocal decision to actually do something about your situation, beyond complaining and feeling sorry for yourself.

If you don't move forward but retreat, you're just perpetuating your own patterns, the cycle of dysfunction, the patterns that you have built for years and years and have gotten you to where you are today.

Stop finding love and appreciation and connecting through complaining. Exercise trying to connect with other people through possibility, love, success and positivism. If you do I guarantee your life will dramatically change.

Commit to doing something extraordinary with your life. Make the decision to leave all that negativity behind.

Ask yourself:
1) What is the unequivocal decision I have to make for myself?

2) How can I relate to people through success, positivism,

love and possibilities?

3) Where do I need to go to find these people?

4) What do I need to do next to give myself permission to shine and to become the best version of myself?

CHAPTER NINE
ARE YOU WILLING?

"It doesn't matter that you want it. What really matters is how much you want it. The extent and complexity of the problem does not matter as much as does the willingness to solve it."
- Ralph Marston

Change is not easy.

Success is not easy.

Building a business is not easy.

Upgrading your life is not easy.

Unfortunately the greatest pushback you will experience in the journey to freedom and success will come from the people closest to you - your parents, your husband, your children, your friends, and your extended family.

The difference between people who succeed in life and people who don't boils down to one thing and one thing only: Those who succeed have a willingness to do whatever it takes to overcome any obstacles or challenges that are put in their way.

In the decision to see the challenge, move and work around it to continue moving forward in the direction that you truly want to go. Easy? No. Fundamental? Always!

You may have certainly experienced the fact that everyone will tell you they want to experience success. Everyone wants to have more money. Everyone says they are ready to live a better life. Everyone will vow to lose weight, stop smoking, stop drinking, exercise more in the new year… every year. Unfortunately very few will ever achieve their goals. Why? Because very few people are willing to put in the work, dedication, commitment and discipline needed to make those dreams and aspirations a reality.

Very few people are willing to do what is required of them. Very few are willing to get uncomfortable, overcome their fears and their insecurities in the name of what they said they wanted. Talking is easy. Dreaming is easy, too. Doing the work is rarely easy.

Things do not always come easy to us. Success is not an easy path, and starting, growing and maintaining a successful business is not as simple as it appears. Life has its challenges. Growing and evolving inevitably involves a level of discomfort, pain or suffering.

The best you can do for yourself is start the journey understanding that it is most likely not going to be a walk in the park. In fact, it's going to be difficult, and there'll certainly be rough patches and challenges.

During those times, you have to be willing to go the extra mile – perhaps waking up a little earlier that day, going to sleep a little later, or even working on the weekends. You may have to travel to a conference, hire a mentor, or invest in a program. In short, you'll have to be committed to doing whatever it takes to surmount your particular challenges.

If you need to attend a networking meeting and you don't have anybody to leave your children with, you may have to arrange childcare. If you have no money to invest in getting the business started and hiring a mentor, well, you either go get a job or get a loan to which you are committed to repaying. If the people around you do not believe you should go after what you want, you either give up on your dream and betray yourself, or ignore their opinions and follow your heart.

There is a wonderful quote I love: "It is better to be at war with the world while following your heart, than following the ways of the world and being at battle with yourself."

Whatever your circumstances, if you truly want to achieve that success, or lose that weight, or make that money, or save your marriage, or what ever your goal is, you have to be willing to do the necessary work. You ought to be willing to overcome the obstacles that will inevitably come your way.

In the end, all that matters is that you are willing to move forward in your life. Or are you going to give up when the going gets rough?

Will you focus on all the reasons why you can't? Or will you choose to focus on all the reasons why you MUST?

Let me tell you, there are going to be plenty of situations that are going to show up in which you will be tempted to stop because it's just too hard or painful to continue. And in those moments the question you must ask yourself is: Am I willing to commit to my objectives? More importantly, is what I want important enough for me to overcome my own discomfort? Is _____ (my objective) more important than feeling comfortable and safe?

In my particular situation, this question has arisen in many different contexts at various times in my life. I believe one of the most challenging incidences was one day when I wanted to take a particular training session.

I spoke about it with my husband and said to him, "This is the training that I want to do, this is why it's important for me, and this is what I will do with it." I needed both his financial and emotional support. My training included traveling and leaving the kids and him for a few days. He looked directly at me and emphatically stated, "No, I do not believe you should do it. So the answer is no."

Beyond the Lies.

As I mentioned to you, the greatest resistance you will face when you're trying to change your life, yourself, or your business will come from the people closest to you. That could mean your parents, your husband or partner, or even your children, your friends or your extended family.

In my experience, the reason why our loved ones object to our plans is two-fold. One is because they are used to the status quo, and it's comfortable for them. You see, being who you are today brings a sense of stability and familiarity to everyone around you. No one wants you to rock the boat. Most of the time what is going through their minds is that, after all, you are the one who wants to change, not them.

The people around you may even get fearful of losing you because if you change, you might not want to be with them or care for them in the same way anymore. Naturally, then, your desire to change represents a big risk for them. Their rationale is: why rock the boat when things are fine the way they are?

The second reason is because they truly don't understand the process or why it is so important to you to follow your dreams. They don't understand because they are not in your shoes. It is you who is expecting them to see the world through your eyes, with your thinking and your consciousness. Guess what. That is impossible. They will see the situation from THEIR perspective, not yours. They will reflect based on their consciousness, not yours, and they will deem a situation positive or negative, risky or safe based on their own experiences, beliefs and objectives, not yours.

Often when we want to change or we want to do something, we start reading books, going to seminars, or enrolling in programs. Whatever your chosen course of action is, the truth is you change through the process. You transform through the process. Maybe you did something as simple as going to see a therapist or a counselor. Maybe you read a book or just listened to a couple of CDs. Whatever your process of change has been, you have gone through the transformation; and your loved ones and your closest friends haven't. Thus they cannot understand the new world you live in.

The faster you understand this concept, the easier it will be for you to not sink into judgment or resentment for not being supported. The faster you understand those people are still living an old paradigm, the sooner you will know that what is old to you is very real to them.

In my case, I knew that my husband said no, not because he didn't want me to experience great things but because, for one thing, he believed that was not the time to take action; and secondly, he believed that I probably didn't need it as much as I knew I did (This was his lack of understanding.)

His robust NO was uncomfortable and heartbreaking. My desire to change presented a challenge to us, not only financially but on a personal level. It meant the entire family, including our children, had to make sacrifices concerning time, energy, and my lack of availability to them. And frankly, my husband didn't realize the importance of my dream, and therefore, was initially unwilling to make the necessary accommodations.

I really had come to a place of "no return." I said to myself, "Okay, Erika, this is one of those moments in your life which will define your destiny. This is one of those moments in which you're either going to move forward or you're going to stay stuck. Which are you going to choose?"

Before even having that conversation with him, I had the sense he would say no, so even before entering the conversation I asked myself, "What do you think that he's going to say, Erika?" With my answer came my decision regarding what would I do and how I would react in the face of his "no."

You see, you need to make a decision about what you will do in spite of what other people think or believe. Your dreams, future, and destiny cannot be once again put into someone else's hands, or you will never reach your goals.

So I approached him with a thought-out rational argument. "Listen," I said, "This is a program I need and want to do if I am going to reach my goals. Here are the reasons why I want to do it., This is how I plan to pay for it, and this is exactly what I'm going to do. Now, if you don't want me to do it, you will have to divorce me." I just laid it out there on the table.

And then I just kept quiet. He stared at me, and he couldn't believe what I had just said. I didn't say anything else after that. I left, so he had time to think about what I had just said.

At some point – after a couple of days – he simply came back with "Okay, just do it, because I guess you're not asking for permission."

I said, "No, I'm not. I'm going to do this because this is my life-long desire and purpose, and I'm going to do it with or without you. Now I would love for you to be with me because I love you deeply, but I'm going to do it anyway. Even if you do not want to get on the train ride with me, I am going."

I truly have to tell you that that moment marked a turning point in our relationship and set the foundation for years to come. Initially it was very difficult because I was extremely afraid. I did not want to break up my family, but I also knew I could not continue to live my life the way I had been living it during the precious years.

The truth is he may have decided to leave. He may have filed for divorce, and I had to be willing to see that through. So

Beyond the Lies.

whatever it is that you want to create, if it's your true heart's desire and if you're clear that is what you want, if you know that if you don't do that, you will die a little bit inside, then you have to pursue your dreams no matter what.

Moreover, you have to be prepared to accept the fact that the people around you – those closest to you - will probably disagree with your decision. They may be angry and even verbally attack your position, so you need to decide in advance how you will handle it. You must even be prepared for those relationships to end, if need be.

The truth is that no matter what new project you decide to embark upon, whether the change is starting your own business or enrolling in a new program, that process is not going to bring or create new issues in your relationships; it will just enhance the issues that are already present. In my situation, the disagreements we had weren't created because of what I was going to do. They were present because we already had a certain dynamic in our relationship whereby I had allowed him to make decisions on my behalf. Several times in the past I had allowed him to decide for me, to decide whether something I wanted to do was okay or not. That was a dynamic that surfaced not because of my business or my desire to change my existing situation but because those dynamics were there way before the business itself. Most likely this will be the same for you.

That is why you have to be willing to do what you are called to do, even if people oppose you. You must be willing to stand up for what you need and want in order to grow and thrive, in order to live the life you want to live, even if it means you losing something in the process. For you to succeed, your endeavor has to be that important.

Many times I tell my clients, "You need to go about your objective as if your next breath depended on that decision. You have to want it that badly. In order for you to succeed, you need to want it as much as you want to breathe.

When you want your success, as much as you want to breathe, then that day you will be successful, not before and not after.

Stick to your plan. The process of changing your life, your business, or your circumstances is the process of having a healthy ego. Commit to your dreams and your objectives before committing to anyone else's.

Now, it's your turn. The only question remaining is:
Are you willing?

Beyond the Lies.

LET'S RECAP:

The difference between people who succeed in life and people who don't boils down to one thing and one thing only. It is the willingness to do whatever it takes to overcome any obstacles or challenges that are put in their way.

Life has its challenges, and growing and evolving inevitably involves a level of discomfort, pain or suffering, and you have to be committed to doing whatever it takes to surmount your particular challenges.

In the end, all that matters is that you are willing to move forward in your life. Or are you going to give up when the going gets rough?

Will you focus on all the reasons why you can't? Or will you choose to focus on all the reasons why you MUST?

So whatever it is that you want to create, if it's your true heart's desire and if you're clear that if you don't do that you will die a little bit inside, then you have to pursue your dreams no matter what.

Ask yourself:

1) How should I approach the situation with the other party?

2) What decision do I want to make?

3) What decision will I make if they say no?

Stick to your plan, and never give up. The process of changing your life is the process of having a healthy ego and committing to your dreams and your objectives before committing to anyone else's.

You need to go about following your dream as if your next breath depended on that decision. You have to want it that badly. In order for you to succeed, you need to want it as much as you want to breathe.

When you want your success, as much as you want to breathe, then that day you will be successful, not before and not after.

CHAPTER TEN
COMMITMENT

"It was character that got us out of bed, commitment that moved us into action, and discipline that enabled us to follow through."
Zig Ziglar

Commitment is basically honoring your words or doing what you said you would do when you said you would do it. It's as simple and yet as difficult as that.

Many people are compelled to find different definitions for the word 'commitment,' but the truth is that there are not many variations of it. You either do what you said you would do by a certain time, or you don't.

This concept is tricky, however, because sometimes keeping your word is not easy. But when you actually show up and do what you said you would do, you'll see that it makes a big difference in your life and in other's lives, as well. In fact, it is the way in which we build trust, not only how the people around us learn to trust us, but most importantly how you build your confidence and learn to trust yourself.

By making a commitment, you allow others to trust you, but most importantly, you learn to trust yourself. When you honor your commitment to someone or something, you build your character and your self-esteem.

To summarize, commitment is doing what you said you would do by the moment you said you would do it. It means staying true to your word no matter what.

There are many subcategories for commitment, of course, and as with all concepts, there are also many degrees of commitment as well. Commitment can mean different things to different people, and complications can occur when you try to keep your word.

The rigors of daily life get in the way of honoring your commitment. For instance, unexpected events occur beyond your control: you become tired, somebody has a problem you need to solve, your child gets sick, there is traffic on the highway, the milk spills in the morning, your mother is in the hospital, and so on.

The point is that things happen all the time to disrupt our little routines, and it is like that for every human being on this planet. In truth, all those unexpected things are part of being alive.

Although we are all unique, we are the same in that we all go through the same experiences which help us evolve. The only difference between one individual and another is their reactions to things that happen to them. The difference lies in recognizing if you are someone who regularly plans for the unexpected and can adapt in the face of it, or you are the one who deals with situations as they arise. Are you going to do what you said you were going to do, or will you find reasons not to do it?

In fact, will you show up for the task, or are you going to fail?

One of my mentors said that at the end of the day, you can only have results or excuses. Which would you rather have?

That is the only decision you need to make - who you will be at the end of the day. Who will you be and what decisions will you make in the face of adversity?

When you look at yourself in the mirror, what do you see? Do you see someone who overcame the difficulties and obstacles that life presented and made things work? Or do you see someone who finds reasons and excuses for why things could not be done?

Yes, I realize that there are going to be times where you can't show up. We cannot always do what we say we are going to do since there are times when this is not humanly possible.

But at such times, you must do two things. One is to communicate with the party to whom you made the commitment and communicate with this person(s) <u>before the deadline</u> of your commitment. This is called proactive communication.

Second, after you know you won't be able to keep your commitment, you have to make a choice. You are either going to recommit or decide to break the initial commitment.

It looks something like this:

Option 1) "I realize I will not be able to __X__, by __Y__ time. That is why I am reaching out and letting you know what happened, and I am also letting you know that the same thing will be done by ___Y___ (new time frame, same commitment as before)"

Option 2) "I realize I said I would do ___X____ by ____Y____. Unfortunately I am not able to fulfill that commitment, and I am taking full responsibility for the consequences of not fulfilling my promises. I also want to let you know I will no longer be able to do ___X____ at all. Is there any other way I can support you moving forward?"

It is important to notice that no matter what option you take, once you realize you won't be able to meet your commitment, the communication needs to be proactive. If the communication happens after the deadline, then trust is broken, and that is much more difficult to repair.

I strongly believe we all have the right and choice to change our minds. When your circumstances change, or your needs change, you have complete freedom to say, "Yes, I will continue to be committed to this person or task," or "No, this is something that I no longer wish to be committed to." The important thing is to be honest and to have clear communication with the other party.

Unfortunately, most of the time we are eager to please, and therefore it is very easy for us to make commitments to other people. We even go out of our way to honor such commitments, devoting all our time and energy despite our well-being.

On the other hand when the time comes to be true to ourselves, our dreams, and our desires, we often fail to embrace that same level of commitment. It's as if it wasn't as important if we let ourselves down.

We are the first to let ourselves down, whether it is by neglecting our own needs and desires, or simply by not showing up for ourselves. And then we ask why it is that we have no confidence? Why is it that we cannot trust ourselves and our decisions?

What we are truly doing, if we are honest, is abusing ourselves. This is not an easy reality to come to terms with, but unfortunately, it is the truth. The faster we realize it, the faster we will be able to change it. If you do not change it , then that is the fastest way to erode your self-esteem.

The other way in which we let ourselves down is by showing up in the world based on what we believe other people expect from us or need from us, instead of being, saying and doing what we truly want to say, be or do.

We always try to do what our parents, our children, or our husband or partner expect. We think of what our friends want or need from us before we think of ourselves.

In fact, we are often right at the bottom of our list of priorities in life, if we are even on it at all. We forget to ask ourselves, "What do I really want out of life? Which of those expectations that everybody demands of me actually work in my favor?"

So the teaching here is twofold. First, in order to build your business, in order to lose the weight, in order to change your life, in order to achieve whatever objective you want to achieve, you need to first and foremost make a commitment to yourself and your dreams. Put those above anyone else's expectations of you.

Unfortunately, what happens when you put somebody else's expectations before yours ,you wind up living the life somebody else wants you to live instead of the one you truly want to live. Finally one day you wake up, look at yourself in the mirror, or look at the husband you've been married to for 40 years and you ask yourself, "How on earth did I end up like this? Who is this person? What happened? Where did I get it wrong?"

What is even worse is that when you live your life based on other's expectations, you eventually end up bitter and resentful.

However, you must remember one thing - the people around you are not to blame for your choices in life. After all, it's you who accepted the rules or circumstances. It is you who said 'yes' to living that life, whether it was consciously or unconsciously. It was you who made the decisions you made.

We really need to understand that our everyday actions, the way in which we show up every single day of our lives, are crucial to living the kind of life we want. It's easy to forget that hours turn into days, which turn into weeks, months and years, and before you know it, we're much older and our lives are nowhere near as fulfilling as we dreamed they would be.

It is the little everyday actions we take that determine the kind of future we are going to live. I guarantee you that if you are someone who did not show up on time for a meeting because "there was a lot of traffic," then you are probably someone who is often late for your appointments.

Although the reasons may vary, the underlying

problem here could be that you are not planning properly and leaving yourself enough time to get to the places you need to go to. Or perhaps you are cutting your time too short and trying to do too much in the little time you have.

Whatever your situation, the only certainty is that **without commitment, there is no possibility of success.**

I believe that what keeps a person from committing to someone or something is usually fear. At least it is fear when we are talking about committing to something that we do not know the outcome.

When you want to achieve something you have never achieved before, and when you are going through a period of change, there are always a lot of variables. That causes uncertainty, which leads to fear and sometimes even procrastination and self sabotage.

Although some people say they cannot make a commitment because they do not know what to commit to, I believe that that is not true. Some individuals may put off making a commitment because they are expecting a big announcement saying what they are doing is right. They are waiting for the permission of something external telling them that it is okay to go after their dreams.

Beyond the Lies.

They're looking for the parting of the Red Sea, if you will. They are waiting, for example, for some meaningful sign that tells them what their next step should be.

I will talk more about being guided in a few chapters, but for now, let me simply tell you this - **You are always being guided.** You just need to pay attention to the strength and conviction of your inner voice or intuition steering you in the right direction, and you must be true to that 'sign.'

Pay attention to what you hear, what you feel, and what you see, and take action immediately. Whether it be the title of a book that catches your eye, the melody of a song that lingers in your mind, a website that you suddenly are inclined to visit, a friend that calls you out of the blue – whatever it is, pay attention and take action!

If you still do not know what to commit to, I would say start by asking yourself this question: If nothing else mattered, if I was not afraid of what other people would say, or what other people would think, then...

What would I truly like to do?
Who would I truly like to be? *And*
What would I truly like to experience?

And then start your journey; take the first steps. Don't put it off by letting your fear or other obstacles get in the way. Start immediately, even if it is only a small step. I guarantee you, you will be guided through the process, and you will continue to build on each little success you have!

The alternative is to never commit to anything. And when you do not commit, you are failing yourself. In fact, you are deceiving yourself, and letting yourself down. Lack of commitment to oneself is at the root of lack of confidence and self-esteem, as well as all our fears.

After a few years, a person may wake up and suddenly realize he (or she) has lost his inner compass, his sense of self-trust. This lack of confidence causes fear and self-doubt. The individual may wonder, "Why is this happening to me?" Maybe she will come up with no explanation at all. Well, I can tell you that it first started when she did not show up for herself by not *committing* to what she wanted to accomplish.

The consequences of lack of commitment are varied and profound, and these consequences are at the root of our lack of self-worth and self-esteem. And don't even think for a second that there are no consequences when you just wallow in your fears and remain inert. One enormous consequence is giving up on having the life you always dreamed of.

I believe there are many reasons why people do not make commitments. They basically have learned through their peers, through the examples of their parents or the people around them, that it is okay not to honor their word. That if, for example, they are five minutes late for an appointment, it really doesn't matter; it's of no consequence. Or they might try to justify their behavior or account for it in some other way.

In truth, people do not commit because they do not fully understand the consequences of failing to honor their commitments. Usually the consequences of failing to honor our commitments do not happen immediately, but those that do, often do not have extreme consequences.

What people fail to realize is that the consequences of lack of commitment are devastating in the long run. When someone does not commit even in small, everyday situations, you cannot expect them to commit to long-term "important" situations.

The principle behind our actions is what counts. Stealing a dollar from a person is the same as stealing a million dollars from them. At the end of the day, it is still stealing, and you betray your values and yourself in the process.

Being five minutes late is still being late, period, no matter how you put it. In life, you are either early or late. There is no way around it.

When you let yourself down, you lose trust in yourself, and you lose trust in others, too. Not being able to trust other people is just a reflection of your own inability to trust yourself.

Don't fool yourself. The consequences of not committing are serious, and destiny will catch up with you sooner or later.

Commitment to Spiritual Development

Having gone through the Barbara Brennan training program, I decided I wanted to bring those spiritual teachings and the ability to transform one's life to a wider audience. You see, working with human consciousness requires a firm commitment and a phenomenal amount of work since it concerns the energy of both our minds and bodies. It also requires an open mind and heart, and a willingness to do the work involved.

In fact, you need to be a pretty spiritually-oriented person to even be open to the possibility of changing at a cellular level. It is essential to understand the interaction of two human energy fields vibrating at different levels of energy, each influencing the other.

Because I wanted to perform this work on a wider scale, I became a professional certified coach. However, at the end of that process, I was still very unsure as to how to start my business.

I knew that I had this very strong desire to create change in the world, and I knew I wanted to base my work on helping people achieve things they would not achieve on their own. But I truly didn't know where to start or how to get to the point where I could have a consistent monthly income and turn my work into a full-time occupation.

One day, I heard an audio program that a friend of mine gave me as a gift. After attending this person's tele-classes and following his virtual programs for some time, one day he offered me the opportunity to join him at a live event. Because I was very attracted to his teachings, I just knew I had to be at that event.

I went by myself and I simply told my husband, "I need to do this. This is an event I need to attend. I am not really sure why; I just KNOW I have to be there. And this is exactly what I am going to go do."

At the time, my husband didn't fully understand the reasons why I needed to attend this event, but then, I did not even understand them all myself. He just knew that I was extremely motivated to attend the event and that it was imperative that I be there.

This is one of the moments in which I learned to trust my intuition. As we are all aware, there are moments in our lives when we understand at a deep level that our intuition is guiding us in our decisions, and we must listen to that inner voice.

Well, I went to this event - there were probably close to

300 people in the room – and the coach started to address the audience. He began to coach people in the room, explaining and guiding. I distinctly recall sitting in that room in complete awe as to how masterful he was at his craft. I was in awe of the great work that he was doing.

And I also remember saying to myself, "Wow, I want to do what he is doing. It is possible, after all! The ideas and dreams I have are not impossible... they're feasible! There are people out there who are actually putting their dreams into action, and this man appears to be guiding them to affect those major transformations in their lives. Well, if all of them can do it, then I certainly can too!"

I remember saying to myself, "There has to be a way to make this happen."

When I saw him coaching the people in the room, I also remember thinking, "Everything that's coming out of his mouth is brilliant, and he explains things in a way that is just amazing. But you know what? I could do that, too. I have the potential to do exactly what he is doing; I just don't know how to start. So right now, I need to learn."

Then I approached one of the speaker's coaches and said, "Listen, I know I need to study with this person. I don't know how to go about it, though. Could you help me?" She told me that he was going to make an offer to mentor, but that that offer would be at a cost of around $50,000.

Beyond the Lies.

Naturally, I didn't have that amount, so I replied, "Well, I can't do that, but I need to do something. I can't leave this place without taking some sort of action."

Then she told me, "Well, there is another option. In this option, you can attend a smaller event that will take place in around a month-and-a-half. It is a two-and-a-half day event, as well. And there will only be around 25 to 30 people in the room. I believe that this might be your next step." I thought about it - it was a small setting, just perfect for me. Then she added, "If that sounds good to you, then that is exactly what you need to do."

She said it with such conviction that I just knew I had to do it. So I replied, "Yes, definitely, I will do it. Can you tell me what the cost is?"

This is where I struggled with the problem of commitment. Up until then, I had paid for all expenses connected to this first event (which I believe was $197.00 refundable). I had also paid for my hotel, airfare and meals, and the total amount had already proven a challenge. Not only financially, either. Making this sacrifice of time and money challenged my commitment to my growth and development.

I asked her how much the smaller event was, and she replied: "It is $3,000." At that moment I remember feeling like a huge bucket of cold water had been thrown directly on me. I was rendered speechless.

A flurry of thoughts passed through my mind. "Where am I going to get the money from?

How am I going to even pay for this?

Do I even have a credit card with me that I can put this on?

What am I going to learn here?

Is this even good for me, important for my growth?

Am I going to get what I need?"

As I said, there were a thousand questions bouncing around in my mind, and I remember I was literally shaking. In fact, I started crying because the feelings were so overwhelming. Noticing my strong reaction, the woman told me, "Just take a deep breath. Relax. Do you have a credit card that you can put this on?"

At that moment I thought: "Well, I do have one with me, but it cannot hold the whole charge," I thought. "I can divide the payments in three." I also heard a voice inside me saying, "If you pay that amount, the three thousand dollars, the moment you get home you're going to get into the biggest fight of your life."

But you know what? I felt strongly about this, and I was committed. I remember when the instructor was teaching from the stage, and he said, "Every single thing you do towards your next step is going to challenge you to the core of your being, and at that moment you're going to decide your destiny. At

172

Beyond the Lies.

that moment, your destiny will be written."

Many years later, I heard these same words from another speaker, about how our destiny is decided during those crucial moments when we have to make an important decision in our lives. And those words are absolutely true.

Quite often we believe that our destiny is created by magic, out of thin air. We may feel that some random occurrence out of our control happened along the way that brought us to where we are at present.

But nothing could be further from the truth. **Our destiny is decided during those little moments of decision. Our destiny is decided in the small everyday choices we make.** When we choose whether we are going to say 'yes' to an opportunity for growth or 'no'. Depending on that decision, we can predict the results we will see in our lives within a year, in two years, or even five years. It is in those small moments of decision that our destiny is written.

So, as I said, I felt that I was at a crossroads in my life. I could say 'yes' to this amazing opportunity or 'no.' The pressure of this important decision was overwhelming. I began to cry and shake uncontrollably. Ironically, I was warmly dressed in two jackets and a scarf, and also, I was inside a comfortable room.

It was early March, and the event was taking place in

Salt Lake City. Outside it was snowing, but the room was not actually that cold. Nevertheless, I could not stop shaking. What was happening?

Well, the pressure of the decision was making me both nervous and excited at the same time. I reacted by taking out two credit cards from my wallet and saying in a calm and steady voice, "I can give you a down-payment of two-thirds of the cost, and when I get home, I will give you the number on my third credit card."

The woman said, "Okay, I'll take it. That's fine." Part of me couldn't quite believe what I was doing. A different person seemed to be performing this action. But the bottom line is, I paid for it.

I got home, and as predicted, I did get into an argument with my husband. However, it was not as bad as I thought it was going to be. Obviously I had gone through a lot of transformation and growth, and he wasn't there with me to see it happening. So naturally, it was difficult for him to understand why I was doing all this.

I remember I told him, "I'm willing to work the rest of my life to pay for this $3,000. What I'm *not* willing to do is *not* take the next step that I know I need to take."

Beyond the Lies.

So I paid for the upcoming event and attended it. And I can tell you that right from the start, my life was never the same.

What happened as a result of my initial courage to seize the opportunity was that I got what I needed. I got the direction that I needed, and the motivation and inspiration to continue on my journey. As a result, I was transformed in the process - my character, my way of being, and my thinking. With a new enlightened perspective, I was able to take the next step after that.

So understand that every single time you make a decision, especially when that decision is going to take you closer to your ultimate objective, it's going to challenge you to your core.

Yes, it will be uncomfortable and even scary at times, and you will probably experience an immense desire to stop the process and return to your safe, yet stagnant cocoon.

The questions at that moment have to be: "Who are you going to be right now? Are you going to be the person who gives up and tries to find all the reasons why you can't do something? Or are you going to be the kind of individual who rises to the occasion and takes the next step that is in front of you?"

Let me repeat it here because it is really important. It is

in these moments of decision that your destiny is written. All you need to do is to ask yourself, "What do I want my destiny to be?" And then you must make the decision or decisions that support the kind of life you want, the bright future you envision.

LET'S RECAP:

Commitment means showing up for your words and doing what you said you would do when you said you would do it. It's as simple, yet as difficult, as that.

Commitment is the way in which you allow others to trust you, but most importantly, it is the way in which you learn to trust yourself. When you do not let yourself down, you build your character and your self-esteem.

People are eager to commit to other people and often go out of their way to show up for them, but when the time comes to show up for themselves, their dreams and objectives, they are the first to let themselves down.

By doing that, their self-esteem is eroded. Well, we need to change this. We need to put our dreams and objectives as our top priority and show up for ourselves every time. By doing so, we learn to build trust in ourselves.

Beyond the Lies.

Yes, I know that life inevitably gets in the way of our progress. But when it does, try following this two-step process:

Step one: Be proactive and communicate with the person or party you are committed to. Let them know you are aware of what is going on, and be respectful of their time and their life circumstances.

Step two: At the moment you have to make a choice, you either communicate that you will no longer be able to keep your commitment or you decide to recommit to a later date or time.

Remember, you always have the freedom to change your mind, as long as you are honest and communicate it to the other party. It is okay to change your mind as it is part of the commitment to yourself.

Your destiny is decided during those crucial moments of decision.

Who are you going to be at that moment?

Are you going to be the person who tries to find all the reasons why you *can't* do something? Or

Are you going to be the kind of individual who rises to the occasion and takes the next step on the journey?

The choice is yours. Your Life ~ Your Choice.

So start by asking yourself this: if nothing else mattered, if I was not afraid of what other people would say or think, then...

What would I truly like to do?

Who would I truly like to be?

What would I truly like to experience?

CHAPTER ELEVEN
IT IS NOT EASY

**"That which doesn't kill us makes us stronger." -
Friedrich Nietzsche**

We all want more right? We want a better home, a better car, more freedom, more money, more love. Whatever your "more" is, as long as you are alive you will want more. It is just a natural instinct, a feeling of being fully alive.

The problem is that when we want more we forget one of the fundamental principles of having, being, or doing more. Having "MORE" will call us to BE more, to give more, to grow more, and that, my friend, is called change.

Change is rarely easy. Change will get us out of our comfort zone. Change will get us tired, some times exhausted, and will call us, at times, to question why we wanted that "more" in the first place. The biggest mistake you can make is expecting the change, or the journey to "more," to be easy. If you do you will be setting a trap for yourself.

Let's get this straight. Change is NEVER easy.

Change is ALWAYS strenuous.

But it is that journey of struggle which will make you stronger, wiser, and more powerful. It is the journey of struggle that will allow you to have, be, and experience more.

So instead of judging and resisting the struggle, we should start to embrace it and even honor it. It is in recognizing the struggle, accepting and even looking for it, that we welcome that change and that "more" into our lives because, the truth is, it's easier to be in our safe and comfortable ruts than to try to stretch ourselves and feel pain and the discomfort of change.

So I invite you today to make a decision that will most likely change your life. What would you rather be - successful and free, or comfortable and safe? Most of the times those two do not go together, so do yourself a favor and decide.

One of my favorite mentors said to me, "If you are not afraid, you are playing too small. If you are not uncomfortable, you are keeping it too safe. Learn the art of being uncomfortable, and use it as a GPS for growth and success."

He is so right! Being called to a higher life, accepting the calling you feel in your heart, will always be scary, challenging, and uncomfortable, no matter what. So we might as well accept and honor that struggle. We must see and embrace that struggle as a doorway to more life, to more love, and to more freedom.

Beyond the Lies.

Many of us might think of the sacrifices required and the amount of time and money required to achieve what we want. We may even think about stopping or never getting started because "it is too difficult." BIG MISTAKE!

You can only live for so long without embracing your desires and going after your dreams. If you wait too long you will begin to die. A little part of you will be sad. Eventually you will decide you do not want to live like that, and then you will decide to actually go for what you want. So why let all that time go by? Why not start today? The moment is here and NOW.

Why don't we shift our thinking? Why not focus on the actual benefits and rewards we will achieve when we reach our goals rather than focusing on how hard it is today? If we focus on the pain we won't summon the strength to keep going.

Have you ever heard "The Blessing is in the breaking"? Let's focus on the blessing and not on the temporary pain you are experiencing right now.

Remember that whatever situations you're experiencing in your life right now are the byproduct of who you are and who you have been in the past. They are also the sum of your previous decisions and actions.

If you had taken alternative actions, then you would have had different results. Now, if you want different results, your actions will have to change today. Your decisions will need to change today. But of course, that path will present challenges.

Changing will not be easy. It's going to stretch you and challenge you to the core of your being. So instead of being afraid or wanting to quit when that happens, it's better to recognize that that is what will happen, and that it's all right. You might even say to yourself: "Okay, I know why I feel like this. It's because this is a new experience. I know that it's going to challenge me, but I know that this is what I need to do."

We want growth to be easy, without much effort. As a society, we have become accustomed to instant gratification. Whatever we want must come immediately or be at our fingertips.

Indeed, we can access an absurd amount of information in mere seconds on the Internet. Because we have grown used to having our needs met quickly, we want results to come easily and to happen overnight.

Sadly, most people will get discouraged and lose momentum if they don't see results right away.

Well, I am here to tell you that it doesn't happen like that. Life is not a walk in the park. Everything we desire and do takes time to bear fruit. Any changes we effect in our lives

Beyond the Lies.

take time to become entrenched.

In fact, it's taken decades to get to where you are at this moment. Hopefully it's not going to take you even more years to change your life, but it's certainly going to take some time. The amount of time that will take depends on how willing you are to take those first steps.

I know we all want quick and easy results because that's just human nature. I have been guilty of feeling like this also.

The people that I work with are usually like that, too. Many of them want a 'quick fix' or instantaneous results, and sometimes when those results aren't immediately forthcoming, it's a bit frustrating.

Look, I've gone through this process. I transformed my idea of myself, and my idea of what I thought was possible to achieve or do. I started taking a lot of action very quickly.

In my case, change involved starting to study everything that I could get my hands on. I read every book I could on the subject of personal transformation. I took courses on developing a wealth mindset and courses on online marketing. I also attended seminars on sales and learning the art of being an effective sales person. In truth, I have not stopped studying for literally the past twelve years.

When I knew that I wanted to start a business, the first thing I needed to do was to change my belief system. I had to adjust my belief system to include what was possible, what I could do and what I was capable of achieving. That is why I attended those seminars, and I still do.

To this day, one of the big reasons why I am in business is because I love to learn and grow. All that development and learning, all that traveling and experiences are expensive, but I refuse to live my life without them. Therefore one of the big motivators for me to be in business is to be able to keep attending all those events and seminars and to continue to learn and grow every single day.

One of my main motivators is to be the best human being I can be so that I can honor and show the same path to my kids. I can honor and show the journey to the people who will inevitably come after me. And you? What are your reasons?

At the outset, I followed many different programs. I even hired a couple of mentors who could show me the way. I defined the kind of business I wanted to create. I learned about branding and how to market my business, how to put the word out there and attract clients, how to sell programs online and become a great speaker. I studied the basics of creating a website, acquired marketing skills, and learned the art of messaging and closing a sale. In short, I learned everything about putting together a business including hanging up a sign

Beyond the Lies.

that read 'Open for business.'

It is important to say here that I knew I could not do it alone. I knew I needed help, and I realized that the sooner I could learn from other people, the sooner I would advance in my business.

I did not spend countless months creating a website. Instead, I hired someone who would do it for me. I also hired a designer that could help me with my branding, and I engaged a mentor who could help with the designing of my business and show me what worked in the marketplace.

I learned very early on that you buy your way to success. That is, you have to be willing to invest in the right things. You have to be willing to invest in the right mentors so that they can guide you through the process. That way you save endless years of frustration, struggle and being overwhelmed.

At the very beginning, the first thing I did was to look around and find a mentor I could relate to, someone who I believed could take me to where I wanted to go. I overcame my initial doubts and fears and decided to hire people who could assist me, and you know what? That was the best decision I could have made because that assistance helped me move forward much faster than I could have done alone.

The truth of the matter is that it probably saved me years of frustration and false starts.

Today, I see people make a decision to go it alone, and they don't make an initial investment in their enterprise. They wrongly believe that doing everything by themselves will be cheaper in the long run. However, the problem with that line of thinking is that they unintentionally get stuck in a rut and become frustrated when they get poor results.

They can't seem to analyze or understand why they are achieving poor results, and their first thought is that there must be something wrong with them.

Every business goes through different stages. People see other people or businesses implementing certain strategies, and they decide they will do the same. Now when those strategies don't work for them, they can't understand why, and they become frustrated. Thus, these individuals are more prone to giving up.

In business, you have to adopt the right strategy at the right time. It is then that things work, and you achieve success. When you are in business by yourself, it is often very difficult to look "outside of your own situation." What you need is that all-inclusive 'panoramic' view from someone else who can guide you through the process.

Beyond the Lies.

At the beginning of my business, I started to see results as soon as I took action. In fact, I started getting a lot of results and good feedback from the marketplace, from people who wanted what I had to offer and who were willing to invest. Naturally, that motivated me. However, after a few months those initial results started to slow down. The influx diminished.

That is when I started to ask myself, "What happened here? Why is this happening?"

It took me time to understand that sometimes results come in 'waves,' that there are seasons in business as well as in life. I slowly began to realize that results are not immediate and do not come overnight. Rather, they take time to develop.

In business, the results you are experiencing at this time, more likely than not, won't be the result of something you did yesterday. Instead, they are the result of the actions you took some months ago, and in certain cases, they are the fruit of seeds you may have planted many months or even years earlier.

This was a hard lesson to learn at the beginning, but as soon as I understood it, it became so much easier to design my days and my business in a way that allowed me to constantly 'plant seeds' that would come to fruition at different times in the business cycle.

Now those cycles do not only pertain to business. They are also evident in our personal lives.

In fact, as I started developing my business, I also started changing my relationships, the way that I interacted with my husband, children, friends, and colleagues.

Things in my life were going really well for a period of time, and then they got stuck. I started to get frustrated and impatient. But instead of just staying in my rut, I began to focus more on problem-solving. I asked myself, "What am I doing wrong? What am I missing here? Should I be doing something else?"

What I learned in that situation is that when things slow down a bit, it is a sign that you need to step it up a notch. I understood that I had grown a lot but that now I needed to be challenged again. I needed to take the next step in the journey.

Even when I was challenged the first time and I overcame that challenge and felt happy and good about myself, I unconsciously thought that it wasn't going to happen again. I thought that I had everything under control, and even said to myself, "Wow, it was difficult, but I did it. So now I can relax because nothing will ever challenge me again."

Well, guess what? It did, over and over again. And it will happen to you as well. And each time you're challenged, you'll need to go through the whole process once more. The only difference is that you will not be the same person the second time around. Because of your growth and confidence, this new challenge will not seem as big as the earlier ones. It just won't be as challenging or as scary anymore.

Challenges always appear in our lives, and they are opportunities for growth. Let's say that you get into a fight with your husband or you have a business challenge; you may need to make another investment in the business, for example. Perhaps there's another project which involves a new amount of money that you need to invest. Questions about the new challenge inevitably arise. "Is it going to work for me? Is this what I should be doing?" And the whole cycle starts all over again.

After a few challenges like these, I finally began to understand the process. It was like climbing a staircase. You are on one of the steps of the staircase, and realize you've reached a plateau – you're not moving. So you need to take another step up and challenge yourself. You grow, you get results once more, and then guess what? You plateau all over again.

Then, suddenly, that new reality doesn't work anymore, and you need to ascend to the next step to be challenged anew. It happens like that every single time.

For example, at the beginning of my business, I faced a difficult challenge of trying to get my affairs in order and set everything up so that I could actually put up the sign "Open for Business."

I was working on finding the name for my business, defining my mission statement, creating my vision and marketing plan, and defining the clear benefits I would provide my customers. And while I was doing all this, I was also getting out there and finding customers. As soon as everything was ready, I made the "Big Launch," and I started seeing results. I started to get people interested in my enterprise.

After a while, though, I reached a plateau where it felt as if the 'well' had dried up a bit. I then asked myself, "What is going on? What do I need to do to regain momentum?" I asked my mentor the same thing, and he replied, "You have really grown. Both you and your business have evolved, and you have already become used to your current reality. So now is the time to step it up a notch."

For me that meant creating ways in which business owners (myself included) could collaborate to build each other's businesses, find masterminding groups, and create strategic alliances.

And so I did exactly that.

It was once again about getting out of my comfort zone. A part of me wanted to experience more stability. A part of me wanted not to be challenged again. But the truth is that you need to get used to being challenged. Keep it up; step it up a notch every time is the name of the game, in business and in life too.

LET'S RECAP:

Do not expect the journey to be easy, because it won't be.

Do not expect instant success. Results won't happen overnight.

Know that first of all, there is nothing wrong with you or your business. If you have gotten a mentor and are taking the right steps for stage of your business, then you are on the right path. You simply need to summon a combination of willingness, persistence, consistency and commitment. Never stop taking action, the kind of action that will eventually lead to positive results.

Ask yourself these questions:
- Do I have the help I need? Or am I trying to do everything by myself?

- Am I putting my time, energy and effort into those areas in which I excel? Or am I trying to learn other skills that I could very well pay a professional to do in probably half the time and effort?

- Am I taking the right actions and applying the right strategies for each stage of my business?

- Have I hired a mentor, and have I enlisted a support group for my new endeavor?

If the answer to any of the above is 'no,' then you know exactly what you need to do next.

CHAPTER TWELVE

YOU ARE EXACTLY WHERE
YOU NEED TO BE

**"Faith doesn't mean you never doubt.
It only means you never act upon your
doubts."
— *Orson Scott Card***

As human beings, we have learned to develop far too many expectations. We have this preconceived idea of what our 'ideal life' should look like, what our 'ideal mate' should look like, and what our 'ideal business' should be.

While all of these preconceived ideas are a great way to start the journey, more often than not they cause far more headaches and heartaches than we care to admit.

Reality is imperfect. We cannot have a fixed definition of what 'ideal' means and then expect our lives to turn out as we imagined, down to every perfect detail. Naturally, we are disappointed and frustrated when our actual lives don't measure up to that impossible standard.

When envisioning our lives, we need to be flexible. We need to understand what we want and what we would like to experience, but we have to start living in the real world, a world in which we are operating from our concrete vision rather than from our intangible dreams.

193

Of course, having dreams is fine, but those belong to another place of consciousness. In our awakened state, we should create visions in which we allow for less than perfect circumstances. And we must not permit ourselves to feel defeated by those circumstances.

Somehow most of us have this fixed idea of how we would ideally like to be living. We imagine the circumstances that we should be experiencing at this time in our lives.

Unfortunately, we live our lives with a lot of "should." For example, "I should be able to take on this job." "This person should behave like this." Or "My kids should be doing that."

We all carry our "should," or our sense of obligation throughout our lives. This is what we mean by having expectations for others and ourselves. We expect a lot of ourselves, of those around us, and from life itself.

There are many problems that arise as a result of our expectations, and one of the biggest is that most of the time these expectations have not even been addressed.

In fact, most of the time we don't even voice our expectations out loud. We simply assume that other people will know exactly what we expect of them based on our idealized perception of the person in front of us. And when those expectations are not met, we become resentful and frustrated.

It's like when you fall in love with someone. You formulate an idea in your mind about who you expect this person to be based on your own judgments and – if you're honest – based on your own needs and expectations of how that person should behave. The problem is that this idealization lives only in your mind.

We do the same with our lives, of course, and we do the same with our businesses. We say to ourselves, "By now, I should be doing this. I should be at this level or stage. By now, I should be making this much money or have this many customers. By now, I should be able to have no money worries or fears." And the list goes on.

These expectations are the source of frustration and a constant sense of falling short of the ideal. There is a perpetual notion that "I haven't done enough or achieved enough yet" or "I can't be completely happy with what I have because I still have this huge list of things that I need to do." Whenever we feel that way - when we feel frustrated or like we are letting ourselves down - we start to question everything around us.

We start to question if we should be doing a certain thing, or if we should have made a different decision in the past. In my case it went more like this: "Should I really have agreed to relocate? Should I have left my job? Should I have agreed to get married and leave my whole life behind?"

I believe that at some point in time, it boils down to making peace with whatever circumstance we're living in at the moment, whatever decisions we have made in the past. We should focus on making our present work. Focus our energy on what we want to create in the future, rather than dwelling on the past.

Furthermore, we need to understand that we are living according to a divine plan that is guiding us through the whole process.

I strongly believe that there are no coincidences in life. You are where you are at this moment, speaking to the person you're speaking to or crossing someone's path, for a very specific reason.

If you get into an elevator with some people, pay attention. There may be a reason those people are around you. They could represent an opportunity of some sort for you. If you are sitting in a plane across from someone, it is for a reason; so be open to the opportunity to learn and grow.

Everything in this world is interconnected in a very orderly manner. You do not see planets colliding with each other. Everything in the universe follows a very specific order. Your life, your encounters, and the situations you experience are not random occurrences.

Beyond the Lies.

That reminds me of a movie called "Crash." I don't know if you saw it or not. Its basic premise is that whether we realize it or not, we are all interconnected. Everything I do affects you, and whatever you do affects me.

There is a divine plan unfolding in our midst, but what happens is that we often fail to become aware of opportunities to learn and grow. We should ask ourselves: "What am I here to learn at this moment?" or "What is the opportunity in front of me right now?"

The principle of always being alert to the opportunity in a situation may sound very simple, but in practice it is quite difficult. This is especially true when you are living through challenging circumstances. When you are going through a challenge, it is easier to sink into hopelessness, to feel that you will never be able to change your circumstances.

When you are actually able to see opportunities for growth in your life circumstances, then it's always transformational.

Be reassured by the fact that you're exactly where you need to be at this moment in time, and you're experiencing exactly what you're supposed to be experiencing. Your only objective in each of these moments is to be aware of what learning opportunity is present.

Become acutely present. By that I mean, be present to

the meaningful coincidences in life. The psychologist Carl Jung speaks of the concept of synchronicity. For example, someone might approach you and ask if you have read a book by a certain author. Perhaps you don't pay attention at first, but then you attend another event and someone else asks you the same thing. Maybe you even happen to glance in a store window and notice that same book staring right back at you.

That, my friends, is not a mere coincidence. I believe it's the way the spirit communicates with us, of guiding us towards the next important phase, whatever that may be. What you have to be able to do is seize that opportunity, and you cannot do it if you are 'half asleep.' You must be fully aware. You have to listen, and you have to pay attention.

You cannot pretend to have all the answers, and so you have to make peace with that fact. What is important is that you know at a deep level that you are being guided to experience exactly what you are supposed to be experiencing at any given moment.

While you are going through an experience, you will probably not even know why you are experiencing it, but the answers will eventually reveal themselves. While you are going through the experience, your objective is to trust that you are in the right place, learning what you need to learn.

In my particular experience, one of the situations I lived through that reminded me of this concept, of always being

Beyond the Lies.

guided and experiencing exactly what we need to experience, occurred when I was young. When I was growing up, I had a boyfriend in school, and we had been in the same classes since we were both eleven years old.

Obviously we weren't dating at that time. We were just friends. But in sixth grade, he told me he wanted us to become girlfriend and boyfriend. At the time, his proposal seemed comical to me, as I was not even sure what that meant other than having a particular status in each other's lives.

Basically our boyfriend-girlfriend thing consisted of spending our recesses and lunch time together. Now that I reflect back on that period in my life, it felt so sweet and innocent. It made me smile. I can still feel the happiness I was feeling right then.

Once in a while, my 'boyfriend' would grab my hand in school (which wouldn't happen often because it wasn't permitted). That was basically what our relationship consisted of. But the official titles of 'boyfriend' and 'girlfriend' made all the difference in our young minds. It meant we were special to each other. This relationship continued on and off for about three more years.

My boyfriend was the quarterback of one of the football teams and a drummer in his own band. To me, he was a total rock star! I just adored him, and we had a wonderful relationship.

Then my boyfriend went through a growth spurt, and he started to play on a football team with older boys, eighteen-year-olds. Eventually he attracted the attention of a girl older than me, a seventeen-year-old. She pursued him, and eventually he started dating her.

He had been my sweetheart since we were both eleven years old, and now suddenly he was gone. So I decided that there was no reason for me to stay in that school. My friendships weren't as satisfying as they used to be, and of course, my boyfriend was already dating someone else. I didn't like the school, and I didn't like the environment.

I would often complain to my dad about the school. I'd say over and over, "I don't like that school. I just don't like it."

Finally he asked, "What's so wrong with the school, anyways?"

I told him that I did not like the school anymore. The kids were starting to be really mean; the situations that we were experiencing were too sexualized for my taste at the time; and I felt totally out of place.

When he heard that, he said, "Okay, I understand what you are talking about. We'll find another school for you. Don't worry. Just please finish this school year, and I promise we'll find another school for you next year."

I felt so relieved and understood. I was truly grateful for his support in helping me escape that environment. And true to his promise, I went to another school the next year where the environment was totally different, much healthier and much more normal than what I had been used to.

I spent three years in the new school and had totally forgotten about my former boyfriend. I went on with my life. During my last year in high school, though, something happened. One day I had a close friend over to my house, and we began to chat. Just girl talk. Nothing serious. We were very much alike and really enjoyed each other's company. Suddenly we started talking about the past and people we had cared for. I started telling her the story of my old boyfriend who was still on my mind because I had loved him so much.

She simply said, "You should call him."

But I was hesitant, and replied, "No. Why would I call him? He's very likely still dating that other girl. Besides, I don't know where he is or what he's up to, and I don't see any point in calling him."

Truthfully, I had never liked calling boys. I had heard far too often of girls incessantly calling boys they liked, and I did not want to be seen as one of those. But my friend argued with me for a while, and then said, "Listen, if he's still on your mind and in your heart after all these years, you probably should call him.   But, hey, if you don't want to, I understand." I gave it some thought, but I was still unsure. I said, "No, it does not feel right for me, so I do not want to call him."

She said, "Ok, let's drop the subject. Can we order pizza? I am starving. Let's order pizza and watch a movie."

So I said "That's a great idea. Let's do it."

We decided on the pizza, called the pizza place. Soon the order was on its way. We sat down and chose the movie we wanted to watch.

Suddenly, the doorbell rang, and I cried out, "Pizza's here!" I ran to open the door.

To my great surprise, one of my dear friends from my old school was standing there holding the pizza box.

"What are you doing here?" I blurted out, a stunned look on my face. "How come you're working for the pizza place?"

My friend replied that he had been working for this pizza delivery place for the past three months, and he really enjoyed it.

Beyond the Lies.

We proceeded to chat for a while. He updated me on his life, and I told him about mine. Since I had last seen him, I had relocated twice, changed schools, and experienced many other changes.

At that time there was no Facebook and cellphone use was not wide spread, so if people moved away it was harder to stay in contact with them.

At the end of our chat, he said, "Do you mind if I ask you a question?"

So I said, "Of course not. Go ahead."

He asked me if I remembered Robert. (I will call him 'Robert' for now, for confidentiality reasons.)

I said, "Of course. How could I not remember him?"

"What happened between you two?" he asked in a friendly tone.

"Nothing, really," I replied. After our breakup, he went on to date someone else, and I relocated. I haven't even seen him in over three years now. I honestly have no idea what he is up to."

And then he dropped a bombshell. "Well, I need to tell

you that last week I was delivering pizza to this house, and Robert came to the door for the pizza. He asked me about you - if I had seen you or not or if I knew where you lived - and I said that I didn't know.

"Then Robert said that if I ever see you, I should let you know that he is looking for you. He said that he would love to talk to you. He also added that if I saw you or anyone who knew about you, to please ask them to tell you to call him, or let him know where he could find you."

I was frozen with disbelief. How could this just have happened? My girlfriend and I were talking about Robert only an hour before, and here I was talking to my pizza delivery friend about Robert who was looking for me. How was that possible?

I went quiet, not knowing how to respond. Especially because I knew that Robert did not live in the neighborhood where my friend said he had delivered the pizza.

What I *did* know was that Robert's girlfriend lived in that neighborhood. So I began thinking, "How can he be like that? How is it possible that he is in his girlfriend's home, and he is asking about me? Just what is it with this guy?"

To tell you the truth, I was a bit angry. I began making all kinds of silent judgments about him and his behavior.

Beyond the Lies.

I asked my friend "Was he alone, or was he with his girlfriend?" My friend replied that he wasn't sure, that Robert had come to the door alone. He said that he had not seen anyone else. He said that he did, however, hear a lot of male voices in the background.

"Thank you for giving me the message," I said.

And then he said, "If I see him again, would it be okay to tell him I saw you?"

I thought for a moment and then replied, "Yes, I guess it would be all right. You can tell him you saw me. No problem."

We spoke a bit more, and then said our goodbyes. I told this story to my girlfriend, and she could not believe what had just happened. In a sense, I could not believe it either. It was such a strange coincidence! She convinced me to call him.

However, I was reluctant. What if Robert had been at his girlfriend's home when he had seen our mutual friend with the pizza? I was afraid, and I did not want to call. But finally I caved in.

I dialed his number. I knew it by memory even though it had been almost four years since we had last seen each other. He instantly picked up the phone. I said "Hi" and waited. Then

Robert said "Erika?" in a surprised, but warm voice.

The next thing he said kind of put me off balance, but not in a bad way. "I am so glad you called. You know, I've been looking for you. Would you like to meet for coffee? I'm leaving for Boston tomorrow, but I'll be back on Monday. If I pick you up Tuesday at 5:00, would that be okay?"

Once again, I didn't know how to respond. So I replied in the affirmative. "Fantastic!" he exclaimed. "Now give me your address, and I'll see you on Tuesday." I could detect excitement in his voice.

We chatted for a while, and when the call ended, I went to tell my friend. She was ecstatic.

So Robert came by on Tuesday, exactly as he said he would, at 5:00. He was always on time. When he saw me, he beamed and immediately gave me a big hug that felt like it lasted forever.

The long and short of it? We wound up dating for about four years after that, having great experiences, being really happy and learning a lot together.

I asked him about our mutual pizza delivery friend, and whether Robert had been at his girlfriend's house. Robert was indignant. "Of course not! How can you think that?" he said. "I broke up with her more than a year ago. Actually, I was at a friend's house."

I knew this particular friend and knew that he lived in that neighborhood, too, but I had forgotten about it. Robert continued, "We ordered pizza, and we were five guys in all. Every one of us was just too lazy to go to the door for the pizza." He laughed. "So I had to go. I was not happy that I had to pay for the pizza all by myself because they were too lazy, but now I know it was totally worth it." Then he added, with a shake of his head, "Boy, am I glad I did!"

We dated steadily for the next four years, and I have to tell you, it was a beautiful time in my life.

This is just one of many examples to show you that you are divinely guided in your journey through life. You just need to be aware of the signs, to pay attention when you hear someone mention or recommend something.

Finally - take action. Yes, you are guided; yes, you should pay attention, but if you decide not to take action, nothing will happen. At the end, as with everything in this world, it is your choice to act on the opportunity presented to you, or not.

So my questions to you today are: What would you do? How would your decisions change if you KNEW without a shred of a doubt you were being guided? Have you stopped doubting what you are supposed to do next? If you stopped doubting if you could do it or not and just went for it, what exactly would you do?

In one of Matt Damon's movies, he refers to this as being able to have "thirty seconds of insane courage." That is all it takes - thirty seconds of insane courage to say yes, to hire that mentor, to enroll in that school, to ask that man or woman out, to say yes to what you want to do.

So what do you say? Do you think you can summon thirty seconds of insane courage? What would you do if you felt like that?

Beyond the Lies.

LET'S RECAP:

Reality is imperfect. We cannot expect to have a definition of what 'ideal' means, and then expect it to be created exactly as we imagined in every sense. This is what often happens, though, and when it does, we become frustrated and disappointed.

We need to be flexible, to understand what we want and what we would like to experience. We also have to start living in the real world where we must operate in our concrete visions, not in our ethereal dreams.

You cannot have all the answers, and in fact, you do not have to have all the answers. What you need to do is allow yourself to be guided and supported. You need to be open to opportunities that present themselves, either directly or indirectly, and take action.

Just a reminder here: You are where you are at this moment for a very specific reason. Whether you're speaking to a stranger, or only briefly crossing someone's path, pay attention to what happens to you. Pay attention to what someone tells you or recommends you do. Notice the people around you and what they are experiencing. You are in the midst of that situation for a reason.

Seize the opportunity... at every possible turn.

Ask yourself these questions:

What am I here to learn at this moment?

What is the opportunity in front of me now, in this circumstance?

What am I supposed to learn from this situation or from this person?

So what would do you do or say if you had thirty seconds of insane courage? What would you do if you felt like that?

CHAPTER THIRTEEN
OWN YOUR VALUE

**"The man who does not value himself,
cannot value anything or anyone else."
- Ayn Rand**

Starting a business is much more than leasing an office space or putting up a beautiful website. Those things are necessary, but they are definitely not what will make the difference in the business itself.

The most important part of being successful in business, especially when your business is service based, is to be able to fully embrace the value you provide your clients.

Do not give away your services as if you are ashamed to charge people or as if there was something wrong in asking for money in return for services provided.

One of the major roadblocks or challenges that women in particular have is that they are used to giving to others. By making others the priority, they often forget about themselves.

Women show up for other people and offer them endless encouragement and assistance. However, when it comes to valuing themselves - their time, their wishes, their desires, what they truly want - that becomes a real challenge.

This shows up very strongly in business. I would like to take the concept of valuing oneself a step further. We really must learn to fully embrace the power we have as human beings. To do this, we have to understand that every situation we encounter or every interaction we have with another human being - whether it be in our business or in our personal life – affords an opportunity for growth, for you and for the person you have in front of you.

I believe that every single business, no matter the type of business it is, involves helping other people in some way. Businesses are designed to solve problems, provide solutions, and aid mankind.

We must recognize that there is great value in our product, our services, and the manner in which we deliver those services.

The more you embrace the extent to which you can transform your client's life, the more confidence you will have to boldly present your products or services to other people. Why? You will come to understand that when you sell your products or services to others, you're ultimately helping them achieve something. In many cases, you are helping them achieve something bigger than what they initially thought possible.

I believe that so often we focus only on the goal of growing our businesses and becoming financially independent. While this is essential, we don't fully realize all the ramifications of a woman running her own business.

Besides the money coming in, the secondary effects of being financially independent include greater freedom, self-awareness, self-confidence, and self-esteem. There's also personal pride that comes from being able to provide for one's family and to show up for one's kids. There is also a noticeable improvement in personal relationships.

For you to be able to achieve financial freedom, you need to embrace the value you provide your clients. Many times you may be inclined to underestimate the benefits you offer your clients, and in doing so you unintentionally adopt a narrow view. You don't necessarily reflect on all the secondary benefits of the work you are doing. That in itself is a disservice to those prospects you have in front of you.

You need to stop believing that you are simply helping someone lose a few pounds, or if you are a photographer, that you are *Only* taking a family portrait. You must get beyond that narrow thinking and be able to "see the whole picture."

For example, a photographer is helping much more than just taking a picture. If you are a headshot photographer, you are helping someone see herself in a totally new light, in a completely different way than she saw herself before working with you.

You are helping her increase her confidence and her image built. You are helping her bring out the beauty she could not see in herself. You are also helping her build her brand, attract more clients, and present herself more powerfully. You are helping her get more clients and make more money. Now the ramifications of such things can lead to a better school for her children, better relationships with her partners, or just simply more happiness in her life. She will have the motivation to keep moving forward when things get tough... so on and so forth.

What if you came to understand that in the pursuit of your business - the product or services you offer - you are actually putting food on people's tables?   Or you might even be preventing a suicide, averting a divorce, or helping families to avoid homelessness.

We need to understand and embrace the full value of the products or services we are providing.

This is especially true for women. I've seen this situation arise many times where women say, "Well, I want to start this business or I want to offer such and such a product or service," but when it comes time to offer that product or service to their clients or prospects, they start doubting themselves.

Beyond the Lies.

They think, "What if I can't help this person? What if I cannot deliver the promise that I've made?" There are so many "what ifs." I strongly feel that when we doubt the value we're providing to people, to our clients or prospects, we are doing doubting our own inner spirits – and in fact, doubting the presence of God in our lives.

I believe that every single person has a gift, something special to offer to other people and to the world. We are all equipped by nature and our individual talents to help others around us. You didn't receive your gift by mere chance or coincidence. You received your gift or ability to help people and enhance their lives because of a divine plan. Therefore when you doubt your ability to fully provide your service, you're doubting your creator.

The moment I reflected upon this fact was the moment I realized something was wrong in the picture. You see, I believe in a divine plan. I believe in the infinite wisdom of our creator. I believe this planet functions in a very orderly manner. There is perfection all around us. Who am I to doubt the perfection of that plan? I choose not to doubt but to embrace it.

With that realization I decided that every time I was in front of a person, instead of feeling insecure about how to help her or what to say, or doubting if I can even help that person, I would believe in myself and the value I was providing. I MUST embrace my value. I MUST trust my creator and KNOW I can help that person. I am in front of that person to

HELP. My only objective is to figure out how, but when I KNOW I MUST HELP, I immediately know how. That is the magic of this process.

I believe that even if we don't trust ourselves, we should at least be able to trust God or the power of the universe – whatever name you would like to give it. We need to recognize the infinite wisdom of a higher power that gives us a gift and a mission in the world. And that mission is to offer ourselves to the service of humanity, whether it is on a personal level or a professional level by providing a product or service to our clients.

You need to appreciate your value and start seeing that what you're doing is for a reason. Your only objective at this time is to fully commit to what you're doing and to do it to the best of your ability. That's all you need to do at any given moment.

When I was growing up, I always wanted to be a teacher. That was one of my dreams. My father was a teacher for many years. During that time, he changed the things he taught, according to his life experiences and his developing skills. He started teaching English to classmates when he was only sixteen years old, and then he started teaching mathematics. He became an accountant. Then he taught accounting. After he began specializing in tax returns, he taught that particular skill. I believe that as you start evolving in your life journey, you start teaching different things. You start bringing your gifts to the world in a different way.

In my case, I didn't always know that I was going to help women with their businesses. At the very beginning, all I wanted was to help other women become empowered, strong, and confident. I always wanted to help them escape a perceived bondage of limitation, whether it was to other people, to their own emotions, or to their financial circumstances. That's how it all began.

Then as time passed, I started to develop my own business and achieve results. It was then that I truly began to understand at a deeper level how important it was for a woman to be financially independent.

Whether we wish to acknowledge it or not, we live in a physical universe in which money is a big part of the picture. Eventually I began to see how one of the main things that holds women back is their lack of ability to decide how they're going to spend the money they have.

Will they spend it on their own needs whether it is to get an education, find a mentor or start a business? Will it be to provide for their children?

So often I see women asking for permission as to how to spend the family income. This is mainly because they are stay-at-home moms and do not feel they have the right to decide on how to spend the money. In other cases, they are literally told,

"I make the money. I decide how it is going to be spent." I have seen this countless times with the women I have met along the years.

I began to realize just how important it was for women to understand that it's not okay to put their financial destiny in someone else's hands.

Aware of this, I said to myself, "Okay, if I am helping women to become more confident and empowered, I realize that can not happen if they do not become financially independent."

From my point of view, there is no better way to be financially independent than to have your own business. This is because at the end of the day, when you work for a company, even though you may feel you have more security in the short-term, your job is never really secure. Tomorrow your company can decide to lay off people or decide that you are no longer needed, and then you are out of work overnight and without an income.

I strongly believe that women need to start building a solid future for themselves, and that's how I decided to start helping women grow their own businesses.

When I was growing up I saw my mom work countless hours for her company. I would go to sleep, and she would not be home yet I would wake up, and she was asleep because she was so tired. I basically saw her on the weekends.

I know she was doing her best, and I am absolutely thankful she earned such a great living, a living that allowed me to grow up in a beautiful environment and attend some of the best schools in Mexico.

But I missed my mom terribly. In that moment I just wanted her to stay at home with me, but I knew that was not possible.

When I was looking at my mom work like that, I decided I needed to build a different life for myself. I remember daydreaming about the day when I would have my own business. I said, "I will make sure to have a business, to have my own hours, and to be present in my children's lives. I want to be able to attend their school functions when they have them. I want to decide when and how many vacations I take over the years."

I remember saying, "I need to start my own business so when I finally have children I have some sort of financial stability and be able to be with them as much as I can."

Life does not always happen as we expect it to, so when I graduated from college I went to work for a multinational pharmaceutical firm. It was a very rewarding experience, although I remember how miserable I was the first year because we were not entitled to vacation time until we had been with the company for at least a year. Once you had worked a year, you got a fabulous ten days of vacation for the whole year.

There were tons and tons of rules. You needed to be there by 8:00 a.m. sharp. There was no possible way to leave before 5:00, and even then, if you left before 7:00, you were seen as leaving early and as someone who "did not care" but was just waiting for the moment to leave.

I needed to be in my desk at all times. Of course I could come and go in the building from meeting to meeting, but forget about stepping out to run an errand or leave the office for a few hours during the day to do something. Thank goodness I had no children when I was working a corporate job.

It was insane. I was frustrated, and I was not happy. But everything else in my job was wonderful. I loved the company. I really liked my co-workers. The money was good and steady, and the comfort of a steady paycheck was satisfying. I told myself, "It is not that bad," and I got used to it. The following years were not that bad. I had become used to my new reality. I had become domesticated.

Nevertheless when I had my children, everything changed. I could not stand the thought of staying away from them when they were small babies, and then my desire to have my own business was re-born. I once again found that flame I had

Beyond the Lies.

always had inside of me.

I decided it was not okay to stay quiet about the things that mattered to me. My financial freedom was really important, but it had to be on my own terms, not on anyone else's.

I made the decision that I needed to create a business that set me free to "live life on my own terms," to be the owner and control of my time and decisions.

Is it easier to have a job? I absolutely believe it is - until it is not.

Being an entrepreneur is not for everyone. If what you want is stability and security, I would advise you would to get a 9-5 job. Maybe like me, you learned to swallow your pride, numb your feelings, and get used to being caged in a wonderful golden cage, but a cage nonetheless.

To be an entrepreneur you have to get used to instability. You have to get used to feeling insecure and uncomfortable, at least in the beginning. You absolutely can make it, but it does not happen overnight, although better advice and mentorship can help you get to your destination faster.

For me, it is absolutely worth it. Most times I work more hours than if I had a job. But I work while I have my children in the other room, or even in the same room that I am in. I can work at the beach; I can work at a café; and I can work while I am at home or when I am halfway across the world. All I need is my laptop and internet access, and I can work.

I work because I choose to, and I work when I want to. The degree of my success is my decision and no one else's.

The best part of all? I know that I am building my company, not someone else's. I know I am working in something I love to do and that I enjoy tremendously, and in the end, it is my choice.

I choose if I want to be successful or not. I choose if I want to work more or not. The choice is mine, and nothing compares to that freedom of choice.

Many times I have heard the phrase "What is it that women want?"

My answer is: Women want the power to choose.

I want to live by choice, and I bet you do, too.

The caveat is that a lot of women are blaming other people for not giving them the choice. They blame them for not "valuing them" or "loving them" enough to let them choose.

You have to understand that living by choice - achieving success and freedom - is something you need to go after. You need to make it happen. You need to fight for it.

Beyond the Lies.

No one will give it to you. No one will give you your freedom or your life.

It is up to you to create it, and be so committed to getting it, that no price is too high to pay.

You have to want that choice and freedom as much as you want to take your very next breath. Then you will find a way to make it happen.

LET'S RECAP:

We really must learn to fully embrace the power we have as human beings. To do this, we have to understand that every situation we encounter or every interaction we have with another human being - whether it be in our business or in our personal life – affords an opportunity for growth for you and for the person in front of you.

The more you embrace the extent to which you can transform your client's life, the more confidence you will have as a human being to be able to boldly present your products or services to other people.

Stop underestimating the benefits you bring to your clients. In doing so you are unintentionally doing a disservice to the prospects you have in front of you.

You didn't receive your gift by mere chance or coincidence. You received your gift, or ability to help people or enhance their lives, because of a divine plan. Therefore when you doubt your ability to fully provide your service, you doubt your creator.

So let's answer these questions:

1) What is the product or service you provide?

_____

2)   What are the benefits your product or service brings to your client?

_____

3)   What are the secondary benefits your client can experience as a result of the main benefits (think relationships, health, wisdom, peace, just to name a few)?

_____

_____

4)   Are there any tertiary benefits that will result because of the secondary benefits?

---

5)   How would your approach change if you truly embraced the fact that you were there to deliver exactly what the other human being needed, and you embraced your capacity to do it?

CHAPTER FOURTEEN
BOUNDARIES

"Boundaries define you. They define what is and isn't you. Boundaries lead to a sense of ownership. They allow people to take responsibility, and responsibility leads to FREEDOM."
- Henry Cloud

THE STORY OF ELIZABETH

(The details of these stories and the names of the characters have been changed to protect the characters.)

It was a Thursday morning, at the beginning of November. We were getting closer to the end of the year, that moment in which we start to feel nostalgia for another year going by.

I was in my office after a morning workout. I love to exercise as early as possible because that is when I have the most energy and motivation. I find that as the day goes by my ability to have a strenuous workout diminishes considerably.

Suddenly there was a message from a dear friend of mine in my inbox.. The message read: Can you help?

Puzzled, I opened the email. My friend, who I will call Sarah for now, was writing to me in a desperate cry for help, not for herself, but for a dear friend of hers.

"Erika," she said. "I know you helped my daughter when she had gone through difficult times. That is why I am writing to you. My friend, Elizabeth, is in a precarious situation. She is going through a divorce. After seventeen years of marriage, she recently found out that her husband had another family for over ten years. She has been laid off from her second job. She declared bankruptcy some months ago, and her house is about to go into foreclosure. She mentions she wants to start a business, but she has no idea how to start. I am worried, and I see her sinking a little more each day. Can you talk to her to see if you can help?"

I thought, "Couldn't she have called me a little earlier? Couldn't she have called me when things were not going so wrong? Why do people wait so long?"

There's no way to change the past, so I hit reply.

"Dear Sarah. I will be happy to have a conversation with your friend and see if there is any way I can help her. Have her call me today at 4:45 p.m.

Love,
Erika"

Beyond the Lies.

Elizabeth called exactly at 4:45 p.m. "Excellent sign," I thought. "At least she is interested. Let's see how this goes."

She started to tell me what she was going through. She had never been in business before, and although she had a great desire to be in business, she had no clue as to how to get started. I started to ask some questions, and then I had the rest of the picture. She was in a very difficult situation in her life. She was over 50 years old, and she had filed for bankruptcy eight months prior to our conversation. Her house was very close to going into foreclosure, and she was in the process of signing the divorce papers. She had been married for seventeen years to a man with whom she had two children - one already in college, and the other about to enter college.

When Elizabeth first came to me, she had a lot of personal issues and financial problems.

She used to be a high-performing executive in the companies she had worked for. In one company she was let go because the company downsized. After that, she went to work for another company, and she rose to a management position in sales. But then this company went out of business, so she ended up jobless once again.

She was also going through a divorce. She had found out that her husband, who she thought she knew so well, had another family. In fact, he had had this other family for over ten years, and it included two children with another woman.

Naturally, Elizabeth was at a very low point in her life, and her self-esteem and self-confidence had taken a severe beating. When we started working together one of the biggest issues that she had was that because she had been married for such a long time, she was so used to putting everybody else's needs and desires before her own. She did this even though she had been a professional career woman.

Elizabeth was at the bottom of her own list of priorities. Her needs always came after those of her husband and children, if they were met at all. After her husband's needs were satisfied, the children had to be attended to – their activities, shopping for them, doctor's visits, and so on. Lastly Elizabeth fulfilled her own wants and needs.

One of the biggest things that Elizabeth and I worked on together was setting up her boundaries and getting clear as to what she was willing to do for those around her without feeling guilty or limiting her involvement.

The truth is that her children were practically grown adults, and she was getting a divorce from her husband. So she didn't need to cater to anyone else anymore, unless she decided to, of course.

I remember one particular session we had around Christmas time. We were talking on the phone, and she was literally in tears, crying her heart out. She was feeling horrible because, throughout her married life, she had been able to buy a certain number of gifts for the children, but this year she didn't have the money to splurge on them.

This made Elizabeth sad, and she felt guilty about this, too. She thought, "Oh my God, my kids are going to be mad at me, and they're going to believe I do not love them as much. They're going to think I'm a terrible mother."

She actually confessed that she was considering putting $1,500 onto a credit card just to buy them the gifts they wanted and were expecting from her. Obviously we worked for quite a while on this issue. I helped her see that although, as their mother, it was her duty to be emotionally present and available to help her children, they were almost adults. As a result,, it was neither her responsibility nor obligation to provide gifts in excess of what she could afford.

On top of that, I explained to Elizabeth that her love as a mother did not have to be measured by the number of gifts she gave to her son or daughter. She could, in fact, create other memories and experiences with her children in order to convey her love for them. It was she who had trained and taught those people around her how to treat her.

What really amazed me was that this was a woman who was over fifty years old, a professional career woman and mother. I asked her, "Do you know what boundaries are?" She paused for a second and then said, "Well, I'm not really sure what you're talking about."

I had to explain to her what boundaries are, and the analogy that I used is the analogy of a house. I said, "Listen, think of you and your life as a house. There is a certain amount of property that borders your home. Maybe that property is closed off by a fence or a wall.

"Everything that's beyond that property, outside of it, belongs to other people. It's their responsibility. But everything that's inside that fence or wall is your responsibility. It's yours to protect. Therefore your life, including your business and objectives, lies inside that fence, and that is the 'property' you must protect.

"The structure that separates your property from other people's property is there for you and your neighbors' mutual protection. Think of it as a way of giving each other essential space and privacy. So in the same way that houses and properties have these boundaries, you as a human being have what we call boundaries too."

A lot of people don't establish those borders clearly because they believe that they will be separated from others. They wrongly believe that they will hurt other people in the process of establishing those limits, and they will feel pain and isolation as a result. However, the truth is that boundaries are what allow us to establish healthy relationships with other people. In business, it is impossible to be successful if you are not very clear in your boundaries with yourself and others.

Elizabeth and I did a lot of work together regarding boundaries. We looked at what boundaries meant for her and the kinds of boundaries that she wanted to establish with her children, her ex-husband, and even with her "friends." I mention "friends" because her friends sometimes expected her to go out with them to expensive restaurants, which she couldn't afford. She was ashamed of telling them, "No, I won't be able to go" because she didn't want to be judged and because she was fearful of their reactions.

I believe that in the business world, as entrepreneurs, we really need to establish boundaries.

We need to understand that the moment we become entrepreneurs our time is also money. We cannot simply give of our time and ourselves because eventually it will affect our livelihood.

Time becomes a precious commodity when we are in business. We must be more mindful of how we use it. There are only twenty-four hours in a day, and when we're in business for ourselves, time is our most valuable asset. We need to learn the art of saying 'no,' and we must say it more often. As a result, when we actually do say 'yes,' we are only saying 'yes' to the things that we really want to do.

The problem is that most of us believe that saying 'no' is difficult, and therefore, we become uncomfortable saying it. However, we don't immediately envision all the consequences of saying 'yes.' While some people believe that saying 'no' is more difficult, I honestly believe that saying 'yes' is much more difficult.

Why? Well, because in the end when you agree to things that you don't really want to do or you know you're going to feel resentful, angry or overwhelmed about doing them, the price you pay as a human being and an entrepreneur is far greater than if you simply say, "I'm sorry, but I can't do this. I really wish I could do it, but I can't."

In that moment of refusal, there may be a little bit of discomfort, but a few minutes later, you'll feel much better about your decision. You will have honored your objectives, desires, your business, and ultimately, your life itself. By taking this stand, you will feel a sense of self-respect, and the other individual will respect you as well. This is one of the greatest challenges of every entrepreneur.

Before our work together, Elizabeth never really had time to do anything. She was always rushing through everything she was doing. She was forgetful and didn't accomplish a lot of tasks, and because of that, she wasn't reaching her financial goals. She wasn't growing her business, and she didn't focus her time and energy on the things she really wanted to do. On top of this, she was resentful and angry about not being able to create what she really wanted, and she felt she was trapped.

Elizabeth was living her life as if she had no choice as to how she was going to spend her time and her energy. However, through our work together, Elizabeth began to make major changes in her life.

I gave her a few books and some literature to read, and we also worked through her boundary issues for quite a while. After I helped her to establish her boundaries, she was able to allocate her time much better, and her goals became clearer. Elizabeth was grateful for the time she got to spend with her loved ones because suddenly she was in control and could make her own choices as to how she would spend her time.

She was the one choosing to spend time with them, and she felt good about it. Moreover, Elizabeth could now grow her business because she was focusing and had the energy to actually perform the entrepreneurial tasks that needed to be done. Naturally, she began to see results in her business. She started to attract more clients; she created her brand, and she had the time, energy and motivation to dedicate to her business instead of squandering it on things that were not bringing her results and were leaving her exhausted.

We continued working together for two years. She decided she did not want to live in the big house she had because it didn't make personal nor financial sense. But instead of losing it to foreclosure, she sold it and made some money from the sale.

Working with her and seeing her transform into a confident and successful woman was a true delight. There are very few things as wonderful as helping people in your business, and when you receive a phone call or email from someone thanking you for being a presence in their life, it is very satisfying. There are many things I love about my business, but nothing compares to the satisfaction I feel when I see that I have made a profound difference in someone's life.

Along with being able to establish boundaries comes the 'stop apologizing' philosophy. I strongly believe that women unfortunately have been taught that we should not rely too much on our own opinions and that we should remain quiet. We've learned that we shouldn't be too loud, laugh too much, or attract attention to ourselves in any way. Far too often we even apologize for standing up for what we believe in or really desire. When we do that, we start feeling guilty about putting our dreams and our objectives as a priority.

In the same way that the journey of being a powerful entrepreneur is the challenge of establishing strong boundaries, so too is the challenge of owning your voice. By this I mean getting really clear about what you want, what you don't want, and what your opinion is about the things happening in your business and world.

You need to voice those opinions without apologizing for

what you think or feel or for what you want to do or create. In other words, you have to step into your full power and say, "This is what I want. This is what's truly important to me, and this is what will make me happy. I also know that the minute that I am happy and I am living my life 'in purpose' and by choice, I will be able to be a better human being and better able to enhance the lives of people around me, as well."

When that happens, the first people who will benefit from you being that strong non-apologetic person are those closest to you - your spouse and your children. After that, your friends, clients, the people in your community, and the world will be affected.

What needs to happen is that you have to change your mindset from being unsure about voicing your ideas and opinions, and you must start paying attention to that inner voice that says:

"This is not okay. You need to express yourself."

There is a quote that I love by Martin Luther King, Jr. which says:

"We begin to die the moment we become silent to the things that matter."

I think this is such a powerful quote because it's simply put and absolutely true.

Whenever there is something going on in your personal life, your business, or community that you feel is not right and you don't stand up and say something, there's a part of you that starts dying. You compromise yourself, your core beliefs, and who you are as a human being. When you're silent to the truth, you start to die inside.

We women have to stop apologizing for who we are and be bold enough to take a stand in our lives. We need to know inside that, like the L'Oreal commercial says, we are "worth it."

We need to proclaim, "This is what I want and what I want to create. I am not willing to compromise. I know that when I embrace my full power and live my life 'in purpose' and by choice, I will be a powerful example to the world. Only then will I be able to motivate and lead other people, especially my children and those close to me, to live the life they want to live."

That's what I call "living life on your own terms."

One of the things I like to tell my clients – and it goes hand in hand with establishing boundaries and 'stop apologizing' - is that you need to only embrace the rules that set you free.

Our world is full of so many rules, and most of the time the rules we're following are set by the government, our parents, our families, our husband, our friends, or authority figures. I

Beyond the Lies.

do believe there are certain rules that allow us to live in harmony with each another. So I'm not saying "Go out and step on other people and and transgress other people's boundaries." What I mean is that you must be able to own your truth. Own your truth and ask yourself: "What are the rules by which you want to live your life?"

Please notice that I said 'live *your* life.' Other people don't have to live their lives based on your rules. But you do have a moral obligation to decide what rules you want to adhere to in your own life, and those must be the ones that set you free. When you are free to live life on your own terms, in that moment you can, in turn, set other people free to live life on *their* own terms because you don't need anything from them.

You may want to spend time with them. You may want to love them, or show your appreciation, but because you're complete as a person and in your life, you don't need to take from them. However, you can definitely enhance their lives.

LET'S RECAP:

Everything inside your "fence" is your responsibility. - It's yours to protect. Therefore your life, including your business and objectives, lie inside that fence, and they are the 'property' you must protect.

Boundaries are what allow us to establish healthy relationships with other people. In business it is impossible to be successful if you are not very clear in your boundaries with yourself and with the others.

The moment you become an entrepreneur your time is also money. Time becomes a precious commodity. When we're in business for ourselves, time is our most valuable asset.

While some people believe that saying 'no' is difficult, I believe that saying 'yes' is much more difficult for the consequences it encompasses.

We women have to stop apologizing for who we are and be bold enough to take a stand in our lives. We need to stop wanting other people to "value us" and start valuing ourselves.

1) What are the areas in which you need to establish stronger boundaries for yourself? (i.e. time, money, relationships, sex, religion, health?)

Beyond the Lies.

2) How can you embrace the fact that is easier to say NO than to say YES to something you truly do not want to do?

_____

_____

_____

3) How can you establish better limits with what you do for others?

_____

_____

_____

_____

_____

4) What are the rules you have been following that are detrimental to your life?

_____

_____

_____

5) What are the new rules you will adopt to have a better business and live a better life?

_____

_____

_____

CHAPTER FIFTEEN
STOP LYING TO YOURSELF

"THE AMOUNT OF GROWTH YOU CAN ACHIEVE IS DIRECTLY RELATED TO THE AMOUNT OF TRUTH YOU CAN ACCEPT ABOUT YOURSELF"
- David Neagle

I firmly believe that one of the biggest problems we have in society, with the way we're living, is that we have become numb to what's truly going on in our lives. We'd rather look at the phone or computer screen than have a conversation with a real human being, let alone have a conversation with ourselves.

We believe that "liking" our posts in social media is social interaction, and the truth is that deep inside the human being there is deep sense of isolation and need to be heard, loved and appreciated at a deeper, more real way than through an interaction with an electronic screen.

I heard Anthony Robbins, the nation's #1 life and business strategist say "Social media is to socializing the same as reality TV is to reality." This is so true. So damn true!!! And yet every time you go to a restaurant you see people sharing a meal while looking at their damn phone screens. Seriously??!!

So why do we do it? Is it because of instant gratification, or because in social media we can share our best side. I call this the MASK. You can share your wins, your happy faces, and your adorable family pictures, but that will always have you believing the lie and trying to ignore the darker side of life which are just normal parts of being alive.

When something starts going wrong with our lives, when we become dissatisfied, or when something unsettling is happening, rather than facing the situation and taking action to change it, we tend to ignore it, to pretend it is not happening. Unfortunately we become numb to that process. We learn to accept it and "survive" it. We get used to living with dysfunction, even when it is absolutely clear that it is costing us happiness, peace, and our life in the process.

'Dysfunction' may be a very harsh word, but we get used to what's not working. We learn to accept and to tolerate things, behaviors and situations even though we would never recommend anyone else to accept or tolerate such things. We adapt to the dysfunction rather than committing to change it. Again - BIG MISTAKE.

Beyond the Lies.

Let's imagine for a moment that you have a disagreement with your partner because of money, and all hell breaks loose. You fight and bicker with each other, and you don't speak to each other for some time, maybe even days or weeks. Naturally, you're angry, and he's angry. During that period, there's a lot of turmoil happening in the relationship, and you say to yourself, "I need to find a job" or "I need to be independent" or "I need to be able to make my own decisions."

Then another few days go by, and somehow peace returns. You're at ease again, and suddenly the urge to become independent subsides.

This is an unfortunate cycle for many women. They find a way to survive the tumultuous moments and end up living their lives waiting for the next vacation, the next birthday, celebration or any other pleasant distraction. They are waiting for the moment that they can forget their problems. They start living their lives in expectation, for that little speck of fleeting fulfillment.

You have no idea how many women like this I have encountered throughout the years.

The rest of the year, they simply numb themselves to the

seriousness of their circumstances. To put it another way, it's like they're enduring the long, scorching hot expanse of desert only to anticipate the brief oasis along the way.

It's crucial that we stop lying to ourselves. Unfortunately, most of us lie to ourselves way too often. One thing I learned from my mentor was that *when you lie to yourself, you allow other people to lie to you, too.*

What I would like to do is to wake you up to the reality of your life because that is the only way you will have a slight chance to change it for the better.

If you are reading this book now, I would like to say "Stop lying to yourself." You know that there are temporary distractions that keep you busy and take you away from examining your life more closely. You know it takes guts and willingness to look within, but if you truly want to change and want to wake up to a much better life one day then this is an indispensable exercise.

Beyond the Lies.

So, let me ask you: What is it that is truly happening in your life right now?

And what will you choose to do about it?

Stop gambling with your happiness. Quit playing around, and wake up to the fact that the decisions you make in your life will have consequences. Whether those consequences happen tomorrow or in five years, it doesn't matter. They will eventually occur.

If you have a poor diet, eat a very high content of fat every single day, and don't exercise, eventually you'll have a health-related issue, whether it's high cholesterol, or something more serious like a heart attack or stroke. The only thing you have to decide is whether you're going to prevent it now. Or will you close your eyes and pretend it's not happening until, one day, it really happens. Then you are lying down in a hospital bed or walking around with tons of pills in your pocket just so you can breathe.

Doing something now, although it may be uncomfortable, is not nearly as uncomfortable as experiencing the consequences of our bad judgment and neglect.

Remember my client, Elizabeth, whose husband had a secret family for ten years? She knew the signs. She just didn't want to admit that she knew. She told me, "Erika, I knew it. I felt it in my gut, but I just didn't want to acknowledge it. And today I am 56 years old. I have two children and no money. I am divorced and completely miserable. I just knew all this would happen. I can't believe I did not do anything about it when I could have."

I believe that we women have a moral obligation to stop lying to ourselves. We need to do it not only for ourselves, but for the sake of our children who learn their behavior from us.

In truth, we need to step up and face the truth of our lives, whatever that is, and start rebuilding from there. For instance, starting a business is much more than simply buying the URL, putting up a two-page website, making a phone call, or getting some money coming in. It is about rebuilding our lives.

What we should do every day is to try to improve our lives. Every day when you wake up, you have a decision to make. Are you going to live your life 'on purpose,' or are you going to design your day so that you merely cross off your To Do list?

Beyond the Lies.

Are the actions that you take today going to take you to a better place, or are they going to numb your feelings? Will you pretend that everything's okay when deep inside your soul is dying? That's a decision you need to make every single day.

It may sound dramatic, but it's true. I strongly believe that we are fighting for our lives on a daily basis. Don't be mistaken. You are fighting for your life, especially when you're not living the life you want to live and you're dissatisfied with whatever situation you're experiencing. In this world, you've got to fight for what you want. You have to accept being uncomfortable. You've got to make different choices, and you've got to start taking action. And you can't do all that if you keep lying to yourself.

At heart, it's about being honest with yourself. The more dissatisfied we are with the life we're living, the more difficult it is to be honest with ourselves because it's extremely painful.

It makes us uncomfortable, and that's usually not something we want to feel or experience. We would rather have constant fireworks and rainbows, not a pile of garbage that needs to be cleaned up.

Imagine if you have a beautiful flower garden, and a bunch of weeds crop up to spoil it? Or maybe somebody dumped some garbage all over it. Well, if you don't pull out those weeds or clean up that mess, more weeds will appear and more garbage will accumulate. Then by the time you try to clean it up, it will be more difficult to do so, if not impossible.

Our lives are no different. If you already have an unruly garden, you don't have to pull up all the weeds by tomorrow. You don't have to do everything the next day or next month. Don't look at everything that's not working. **Start with one thing only.** Start with the one thing that is next for you. Choose the issue that's most important to you, and start working on that. Just don't pretend that everything's perfect when the truth is that there's a lot of cleaning up to do.

When I started my journey of transformation about fourteen years ago, I began examining the part of my life that was the most painful and made me unhappy. That part was my personal relationships and the way that my partner and I were handling the issues as a couple. After I started fixing things there, then I began to look more closely at other aspects of my life that I wanted to change. Before I knew it, I was changed, and my life was changed.

Beyond the Lies.

I am going to be honest with you. That process is one that never stops. When you see the power of the change, you fall in love with the process. I started about fourteen years ago, and I have never stopped. It is part of who I am. It is part of what makes me stay in sync with who I am and who I want to be. Now I do it out of pleasure and choice, not so much out of necessity. There are moments and days where I am just grateful to be able to have some people on my speed dial who I can call when things get tough.

Every successful entrepreneur, every successful person on the planet, has a "magic and secret weapon" on speed dial. Some of us have quite a few speed dial "secret weapons." We are human beings, and we need support. We are not perfect even if we try to be. The greatest part of the journey to the top is to not try to do it alone but to embrace the fact that paying for support is a necessary privilege that you cannot afford to do without.

Start somewhere. Look and see what needs changing. What you can't do, though, is close your eyes and pretend everything's fine when you know it's not. That is when you become discouraged, depressed, and in a bad place emotionally because you're not living your life 'on purpose.'

Show me one person who is depressed, and I'll show you a person who's not living a life of purpose. Show me one person who's sad, and I'll show you a person who's not expressing their gift. Show me one person who is emotionally down or angry, and I'll show you a person who's not thriving, who is not able to look within, and who is not able to make quick decisions to make herself a priority in her own life.

The way to get to a good place is to embrace your gifts, design your life, and decide to be honest about the things you want and need to change. Then start taking action. But please, this action needs to happen now – not next month or next year. Not with the next crisis. Not when you wake up one day and, like Elizabeth, you're 56 years old and your life is in a shambles. Your husband has been cheating on you for ten years, and you don't have a cent to your name.

The time to act is now. That's why you're reading this book. That's why we're having this conversation on the page right now. The time is here – to choose your life, your objectives, and first and foremost, to put yourself as your number one priority.

Beyond the Lies.

The time to act is right here and right now. Not next month or next year. Stop pretending you will live forever, and dedicate yourself to live your life to the fullest.

As I am writing this book, I have just received the news that a very close friend of mine has passed away. He was a great man who had overcome many difficulties. He was a great soul and dedicated his life to helping children and talking to teenagers about not going towards numbing drugs and bad habits. He was found in his car murdered as a result of a robbery. I am terribly sorry the world lost such a great person, and it has also made me reflect on the fact that nothing is set in stone.

Your today is all you have. My today is all I have. We need to make it the best that we can. Stop pretending we have fifty years ahead of us to live. I certainly hope you do. I hope I live a long life too, but we simply do not know. The moment is HERE and NOW.

Start with a simple step. Don't feel that you have to do everything all at once. You'll become overwhelmed, and you will want to quit.

Take one step. Open the first door even if it's not perfect.

Because you know what? That first difficult step is the one that is the most important. It's the beginning of your journey of transformation.

At the other side of that door, there is a whole party of people cheering for you, waiting for you to step up to the challenge and join them in the beautiful game that is called life.

When will you decide to open the door? We are waiting for you.

With all my love,
Erika.

Beyond the Lies.

LET'S RECAP:

One of the biggest problems we have in society, with the way we're living, is that we have become numb to what's truly happening.

It's crucial that you stop lying to yourself. When you lie to yourself, you allow other people to lie to you, too.

Stop gambling with your happiness. Quit playing around, and wake up to the fact that whatever decisions you make in your life will have consequences. Whether those consequences happen tomorrow, or in five years, it doesn't matter. They will eventually occur.

We are fighting for our lives on a daily basis. Don't be mistaken. You are fighting for your life every single moment of every single day. Choose the good fight; choose the fight that will set you free, not the fight that will keep you stuck.

Every successful entrepreneur, every successful person on the planet, has a "magic and secret weapon" on speed dial. What do you have?

1. Be true to yourself. What is truly happening in your life right now?

2. What needs to change?

3. What will you choose to do about it?

4. Who is your "secret weapon?" Who is that mentor or ally that you can call at any moment who will help you move forward?

5. Who is the next person you need to hire?

The time to act is right here and right now. Not next month or next year. Stop pretending you will live forever, and dedicate yourself to living this life to the fullest.

At the other side of that door, there is a whole party of people cheering for you, waiting for you to step up to the challenge and join them in the beautiful game that is called life.

When will you decide to open the door?
We are waiting for you.

With all my love,
Erika

WOULD YOU LIKE ADDITIONAL HELP?

We invite you to request Erika's invaluable free training:

Attract More Clients with your Blog
OR
The 7 Biggest Mistakes Every Entrepreneur Makes When Starting Their Business AND How to AVOID Them.

This training is absolutely FREE. All you have to do is request it at:

http://TheUnstoppableFemale.com

and I want to Invite you to Join Our Community of Unstoppable and Unapologetic leaders and Entrepreneurs at:

http://unstoppablefreecommunity.com

If you want support on growing your business and getting more clients check out Erika's Unstoppable Confidence & Profits Club at http://theunstoppablefemale.com/ucpc/

Or scan this image with your mobile phone:

NOTES

Beyond the Lies.

NOTES